The Bride's Guide to

The Wedding Party

The Bride's Guide to

The Wedding Party

Choosing and Using Your Bridesmaids, Groomsmen, and Others To Make YOUR Wedding a Success

Book 5 in *The Wedding Series*

J. Thomas Steele

ISBN-13: 9781975885793

ISBN-10: 1975885791

First Edition

10 9 8 7 6 5 4 3 2 1

Dedication

To All the Brides and Grooms:

You've chosen each other,
may you choose your Wedding Party as wisely.

And

To My Dear Wife, who did.

"Knowledge is of two kinds. We know a subject ourselves, or we know where we can find information upon it."

--Samuel Johnson (1709-1784) English writer, poet, essayist, and lexicographer

Dear Reader,

Thank you for choosing my book to "find information upon it." I wrote this book to be informative, helpful, and entertaining, and trust you will find it so. Again, my sincere thanks for allowing me the honor of helping you choose and use your Wedding Party.

Best Wishes,
J. Thomas Steele

Table of Contents

INTRODUCTION

Congratulations! You're getting married! Now the real work begins . . .

There are around 2.3 million marriages each year in the U.S. alone, and they just don't "happen." Wedding events take careful planning and organization and even if you hire a wedding planner, you still have decisions and preparations to make to create a wedding that is uniquely and personally yours. Most couples in the U.S. set a wedding date a year and a half after their engagement, and though 18 months seems "so far away," believe me, the time flies by! So, how do you get everything planned and accomplished, in full and on time? You and your partner can't-do it alone—you'll need help . . . your Wedding Party.

Remember: You won't have the wedding you want without getting the help you need!

You must choose wisely to create your perfect Wedding Party, and in this book, you will learn how to choose and use these important people to help your wedding dreams come true. Remember: It is the combination of *your* decisions and *their* actions that will determine how successful your wedding will be.

You must understand that these people do *not* have ceremonial positions, but ones with real duties and responsibilities.

Your wedding should be a reflection of your particular style and your selection of members of the Wedding Party should suit your style as well. Perhaps you don't really need six Bridesmaids and six Groomsmen. Perhaps you find three-year-old flower girls and ring bearers cute, but tacky.

It's the 21st Century and much has changed, including many of the traditional roles in weddings. Still, traditions are important, so give them the spin you feel is necessary to make *your* wedding right for you! Remember, the wedding is really about you, the Bride.

It is your responsibility to make it wonderful and memorable for you and your soon-to-be-spouse. And if it is also wonderful and memorable for those attending, then that's icing on the (wedding) cake!

I wrote this book to help you decide whom best to select as members of your Wedding Party, what duties each member traditionally performs, what duties *you* want each of them to perform, and how to use them effectively as a team to get what you want. Perhaps you want each person to do *everything* listed, perhaps only a few things. Every Bride and every wedding is different and it is up to you to decide what is important to you and to your vision of the wedding events.

Of course, you need to share the information in this book with your partner to make certain he chooses the best persons for his Groomsmen, as well as share this with the other members of the Wedding Party too. Trust me on this. Few if any of those you select to be in your Wedding Party, really know what is expected of them, even your dear, old dad—the Father of the Bride!

Oh, everyone may have a vague idea of what those duties are: the Father of the Bride pays for the wedding and makes a speech; the Best Man plans a bachelor party; the Maid of Honor plans the bridal shower; the Groomsmen and Bridesmaids attend their parties and dance at the wedding, etc. However, few realize that these folks have actual duties and responsibilities to help you make your wedding as perfect as it can be. And you need to understand that it's up to you to educate them.

As you read this book and learn the many traditional duties associated with each member of the Wedding Party, you will see the enormity of planning and organizing the wedding events. Though this book is not a wedding planner, it is supplemental to one, concentrating on the Wedding Party as one element, though an important one, of the overall wedding and teaching that if you *don't* use them properly, you, dear Bride, will be responsible for getting it *all* done! Forewarned is forearmed.

However, though this may seem daunting, after you finish this book you will be ready to choose the right people to perform the right tasks to make *your* wedding as perfect as possible!

. . .

Please note that in writing this book I have made certain assumptions:

The Bride and Groom live in the same area;
The Best Man and Maid/Matron of Honor live near the Bride and Groom;
Both the Bride and Groom's parents live in the same area.

If this is NOT the case, then I have assumed that the members of the Wedding Party will get together well in advance of the wedding date to perform their duties. If they cannot arrive far enough in advance of the wedding date, then it is vital that you ask those who are there to assume some of these duties. After all, you have work to be done and a deadline to meet.

In addition, the duties and responsibilities I have presented for each member of the Wedding Party are not exclusive to them and, in fact, may overlap as you choose — for instance, perhaps you want *both* the Best Man and Maid of Honor to collect the cash gifts for you at the reception. Also, many cultural and ethnic customs and religious ceremonies may require additional attendants and duties from the members of the Wedding Party in accordance with those traditions and rites. As well, you and your Groom may have family traditions that you wish the members of the Wedding Party to perform.

Finally, while I am an advocate of DIY for weddings, I recognize that you may need professional advice on wedding planning. If so, you might consider speaking with a local wedding planner or visiting some of the exceptional websites I've listed in the appendices. If you choose to visit local wedding planners, research that person, as you might a doctor, lawyer or any other professional, before you consider hiring them. Find out about some weddings they've planned, ask for references, and then ask the couple how it went. Know too, while experience counts, a relative newcomer might be more eager to please and have a smaller workload, meaning more time to spend with you.

Always get an estimate of their charges, as you can often hire a wedding planner to plan your entire wedding, as just a consultant, or only as a day-of coordinator. Depending on what you want your wedding to be, many Brides find that the monies spent on a consultant are monies *well* spent.

. . .

I have also followed standard conventions for both my convenience in writing this book and yours for reading it. So, for same-sex couples, where possible, I have tried to use gender-neutral terms, such as "The Couple" or "partner."

When I must write "Bride" and "Groom," same-sex couples may simply substitute "First Partner" and "Second Partner." Likewise, references to "Father of the Bride" may become "Father of the First Partner," "Maid of Honor" may become "Man of Honor," etc.

WHAT DOES THE WEDDING PARTY DO?

Short answer: Whatever you want them to do! Or more accurately, whatever you *need* them to do.

Every wedding is unique. At one extreme, if you have a large budget and have hired a wedding coordinator to take care of the majority of the wedding planning, your Wedding Party is left with only some basic duties, like arranging and attending formalwear fittings, picking up out-of-town guests at the airport, addressing invitations, and other ancillary duties.

At the other extreme, if you have a very small budget and plan a "backyard" ceremony and reception, your Wedding Party has a ton of things to do. They may have to do everything from building a riser platform and floral arch for the couple and the officiant, to renting chairs and tables, to creating most or all of the décor, and maybe even baking the wedding cake!

Only you (and your partner) know what you need to do to fulfill your vision of the ceremony and reception. Before you consider the members of your Wedding Party, you need to know what you want and how to go about getting it.

While this book will show you the Wedding Party's traditional duties and responsibilities from which you may then cherry-pick as needed, they will also have those duties you need to have done to make your wedding uniquely yours. Thus, it is your responsibility to know not only what you want, but to choose the right people to perform those duties. They should be people with whom you can share both the joy and the stress of the wedding preparations.

I repeat: You won't have the wedding you want without getting the help you need. However, you need to know *what* you need before you consider choosing the members of your Wedding Party.

(Not quite sure what you need? Don't worry, you'll learn some considerations for your wedding theme, etc. as you read the book.)

WHO ARE THE MEMBERS OF THE WEDDING PARTY?

By most definitions, they are anyone you want to involve in your wedding! Some, like you and your fiancé's parents, are automatic members of the wedding. Others are people you have asked, have accepted, and will act as you and your fiancé's personal attendants. Some may be occasional helpers or those with needed special skills. Others might be very special people in your life that you wish to honor.

However, many consider the actual Wedding Party to be those who "walk the wedding." That is to say, play an active role in the wedding ceremony. Thus, while a Junior or Honorary Groomsman may act as an usher for the event, if he doesn't walk in the processional, stand with the Groom at the altar, etc., then many consider that he is *not* a member of the Wedding Party.

For the purpose of this book, let's use both definitions.

In general, members of the Wedding Party may be grouped into four basic categories, by two sections*:

I.   Those who "walk the wedding:"

      <u>Involuntary Members</u>—those who by relationship to the Bride and Groom are automatic members of the Wedding Party due to family obligation such as the Father and Mother of the Bride, etc.

      <u>Voluntary Members</u>—those you and your fiancé asked and accepted the position, such as the Bridesmaids and Grooms-men.

II.   Those who assist in wedding preparations, but do not directly participate in the wedding ceremony:

      "<u>Volunteer</u>" Attendants—those who assist and make a contribution on an irregular basis or have a special knowledge or skill you need for some aspect of the wedding preparations; often these are siblings, aunts, and uncles, etc. who may help and consider it a family obligation.

Honorary Attendants—those individuals chosen by the Bride and Groom for special recognition, and are often a sibling, grandparent or favorite aunt or uncle.

*Each of these will be discussed in detail later in the book.

Always remember that these people will help determine the success of the ceremony and, particularly, the reception. While some receptions take place at a country club or a posh spa/hotel, most are held at church halls, banquet halls, community centers or backyards. These places are transformed from the mundane to the magical, and it's *your* group of magicians that do it. I've said it before, and I'll repeat it now: choose them wisely!

How Many People Are in a Typical Wedding Party, and Who Are They?

Although the total number of people in your Wedding Party is determined by your budget, venue, and family and religious traditions, the typical wedding has twelve to fourteen people in it.

For a traditional wedding, the members of the Wedding Party actively participating in the ceremony usually include:

The Bride and Groom
The officiant
The Maid/Matron of Honor (Chief Bridesmaid)*
The Best Man (Chief Groomsman)*
The Bridesmaids (attendants)
The Groomsmen (attendants)
The Father of the Bride
The Mother of the Bride
The Father of the Groom
The Mother of the Groom

And, perhaps:

The Ring Bearer
The Flower Girl
The Trainbearer or Page
Candle Lighters
Readers
Junior Bridesmaids
Junior Groomsmen
Ushers
Others—depending on family, cultural, ethnic, and religious traditions

Note: Some of these duties may overlap or be done inclusively, i.e. the junior attendants may act as ushers and/or candle lighters, etc. Also, although the officiant and honorary attendants may be invited to the reception, they are often not traditionally considered members of the Wedding Party.

*Sometimes referred to by the gender-neutral term "Honor Attendant."

. . .

Those who "walk the aisle" or are typically part of the ceremony include:

The primary participants—

+ The Bride and Groom—you and your fiancé.

+ The Best Man—the Chief Groomsman; leader of the Groomsmen and the Grooms confidant.*

+ The Maid or Matron of Honor—the Chief Bridesmaid; leader of the Bridesmaids and your confidant.*

+ The Groomsmen—attendants to the Groom.

+ The Bridesmaids—attendants to the Bride.

+ The Father of the Bride (or other chosen, usually older, male relative)—escorts the Bride in the processional and "gives her away" to the Groom.

+ The officiant (cleric or official) who performs the wedding ceremony.

In the processional, but not standing with the Bride and Groom—

+ The Mother of the Bride.

+ The Father of the Groom.

+ The Mother of the Groom.

+ A flower girl—a young girl who carries a small bouquet or basket of flowers and walks ahead of the Bride at the processional. Sometimes she carries a small basket of flower petals, which she strews before the Bride.

+ A ring bearer—a young boy who carries a decorative pillow that has faux rings attached to it.

+ A trainbearer (also called a "page")—who holds up the long train on a wedding gown (if it has one).

+ Junior Bridesmaids and Groomsmen (who may or may not stand with the Bridesmaids and Groomsmen during the ceremony).

Other participants—

+ Candle lighters—who light the altar candles.

+ Readers—who read select passages from a (usually) religious text or book of poems.

+ Ushers—for larger weddings, these (usually) men are separate from the Groomsmen and escort guests to their seats, pass out wedding programs, etc.

There may also be others, depending on your family, cultural, ethnic, or religious traditions.

Again, while these people make up <u>the participants in the actual wedding ceremony</u>, the term "member of the Wedding Party" may extend to special "honorary members"—family (often the grandparents of The Couple) and particular friends as well.

Others who might or might not be considered members of the Wedding Party (but certainly receive an invitation to the wedding and reception) include:

+ The parents of the flower girl and ring bearer.**

+ The spouses or boyfriends/girlfriends of the Best Man, Maid/Matron of Honor, the Groomsmen and Bridesmaids and the officiant.

+ The parents of any Junior Bridesmaids and Junior Groomsmen.

*Often referred to by the gender-neutral term "Honor Attendants" or "Best Person."

**Usually they don't attend the reception if theirs will be the only younger children there.

THE DECISION-MAKING PROCESS

Decision-making is a life-skill, and each of us makes decisions every day. Most of these are often unconscious decisions that seem of little importance and usually do not carry great consequences. These are mostly thoughtless, "flip a coin"-type of decisions. Coffee or tea? Fries with that burger? and so on.

However, decisions concerning your wedding are *major* decisions with often great and lasting consequences. Everything from choosing the ceremony site, to choosing the reception venue, choosing the vendors, *and especially your Wedding Party* all require cautious decision-making.

Now, you *could* still flip a coin to decide between people for your attendants. You *could* put all of their names in a hat and draw the lucky winners. You *could* listen to the well-meaning suggestions of friends and family. You *could* do any number of things to make your choice quick and easy. You *could*, but don't!

You need to make sensible choices if you truly want the best people in charge of making your wedding dreams a reality. It's your day, and its success will rest, in large part, on your Wedding Party. As Albert Einstein famously said, "God does not play dice with the universe," and neither should you let random chance be a tool for choosing your attendants.

The Seven-Step Solution

> *WARNING:* This section contains behavioral science content!
> (Science? *Really?*—Yep, sorry about this!)

The most used technique for everyday decision-making is to gather some information about the subject/object on your own, and then ask selected others, who either know the subject/object themselves or to whom you can present your information, to make a judgment about both it and how you should respond to it. You then weigh their advice, perhaps asking one or two of them again for their opinion, before making a final decision.

Usually, this simple method works well enough. But you need more when deciding on whom to have in your Wedding Party and the future decisions during preparation for the wedding events. These decisions require thought and careful consideration, and while it is beyond the scope of this book to offer you a general discussion on the differing decision-making processes that have been identified by behavioral science, I have found that the many books and articles on the methods tend to agree on the following basic steps:

1—Recognition of the problem.
Identifying it and considering it in an <u>objective</u> sense.

2—Researching the problem.
Seeking out and gathering information about it. Being as thorough as you need to be, but recognizing that you do not need information overload!

3—Finding solutions, options, and alternatives through a "brainstorming" process.
During which you attempt to digest the information you have uncovered and find some level of understanding. Often asking qualified others for their advice and opinion.

4—Evaluating your solutions, options, and alternatives.
In which you weigh the relative pros and cons of each solution, option, and alternative; determine several best choices based on any relevant criteria. You seek tentative solutions and classify them; then order these classified solutions (#1, #2, #3, etc.). You re-evaluate and reclassify as needed. However, you must be cautious enough to avoid what is termed "paralysis by analysis" whereby you think

about each possible solution in such painstaking detail that you cannot make a decision.

5—Making a decision based on your evaluation.
Deciding if you should act on your choice. If so…

6—Acting on your selection.
In other words, implementing your decision.
Finally,

7—Evaluating your outcome in light of related issues.
Determining if you made the right decision.

[I apologize for the science. However, everything has a process and I wanted to make aware of this one. Besides, this process can be used for decision-making beyond just deciding on wedding event planning and choosing your attendants. How about that? I've provided you with an additional life-skill, at no extra charge!]

The seven steps sound simple, right? *Sound* simple, sure, but it also sounds daunting!

I know that this seems a lot for you to do (and it is), so it is important that you remember that most of your wedding-related decisions will be accomplished through <u>group participation</u>. Your family and other members of the Wedding Party will certainly help with research and offer choices and opinions on things like vendors, décor, etc. So even though the final decision on all pertinent matters will be yours alone (well, yours and your partner's), you will have input from others to help you explore various opinions and viewpoints as you come to make a decision. That is one very important reason to choose your team wisely—you want the best opinions from the best people!

A Practical Example

Although we will further explore some considerations in choosing these "best people" in the next chapter, let's use the bare-bones decision-making process described above in a practical example, for, perhaps, one of the most important decisions you will make: selecting a Chief Bridesmaid or Chief Groomsman.

Note: For this example, we must assume that you have already chosen a group of Bridesmaids and Groomsmen candidates and that you are choosing your chiefs from amongst this group.

Following the steps above:

1—Recognize the problem.
You already have an idea of the projects your attendants must do, the timeline for the completion of each project, the wedding/reception preparations that must organized and assisted with, etc. Now you need someone who can help see that everything gets accomplished. You need someone to supervise, manage, and lead your chosen attendants.

2—Research the problem.

Some of the criteria to consider amongst your chosen attendants may be family members and close friends who display the following characteristics: they are friendly; work well with others; are dynamic enough to lead; have some organization skills; display maturity; are able to keep secrets; etc. No one person usually has all these characteristics, so ask yourself, "How many of these people have _most_ of what I am looking for in a leader and can this person be a _personal_ confidant to me?"

3—Find solutions.

An easy way to see the process is to liken it to a job interview. After all, there are real duties and responsibilities to perform and you need to have the right person managing to see that your vision for the wedding is fulfilled. Simply conduct an imaginary interview with your candidate and think of their answers to questions about their qualifications. Perhaps use a "mind-mapping"-style technique for each possible candidate. Also, asking others (especially disinterested third parties who know the person) for an opinion may help you make your selections.

4—Evaluate solutions.

Weigh the pros, cons, and relative merits of each candidate. Make a short list and classify your choices (you should have a top three, at least). This won't be easy, but you are the boss of this enterprise and you need to make the hard, executive decisions!

Remember: your first choice may decline, so it is important to have an alternate who is _equally qualified_.

5—Make a decision.

Double check and finalize your short list. Maybe you think about it and #2 becomes #3, and #3 becomes #1! Decide on a top choice and . . .

6—Implement your decision.

Ask them! Explain what you expect from them.

7—Evaluate your outcome.

If they say "yes" and agree to the commitment and work involved, your task is complete. Congratulate them and yourself! If they politely decline, thank them and move on to the second person on your list.

Okay, there is more to the process than that (as you'll read in the following chapters) and I know that the process appears cold, clinical, and a lot of work, but really—that's as it should be! You have work that needs to be done and a decision to make, and you can't let your emotions override your better judgment. You may have to step on a few toes to get the wedding you want, but that's okay because: this *is* YOUR wedding! An upset friend or family member now is better than a ruined wedding.

As you will discover as you proceed with your wedding plans, family and small-group dynamics will play a large part in the efficiency with which you achieve what you need to do. It is well beyond the scope of this book to detail all that is involved. However, your considered and deliberate choices *now* will save you a lot of problems in the future.

Your Decision-Making Team

As I have mentioned, you (and your fiancé) are responsible for any final decisions; but, thankfully—and other than choosing the members of your Wedding Party—you are able to make most decisions through group participation. Your Wedding Party is the committee that makes its recommendations, insights, and opinions known to you and makes your aware of all of your options before you have to make a final decision. They are the ones calling for prices, availability of items, etc. They are the research and development staff regarding your wedding. They are the ones you trust to take care of the "little details."

The people in that group will vary in number as the planning progresses. Initially, it will be just you and your fiancé. Then you two and both of your parents become the team that will determine your wedding and reception budget, and the initial selection of choices for both your wedding and reception venues. Eventually, your team becomes all of you, plus your chosen attendants, and, perhaps, even a few other family members and friends.

As noted, after you make some initial decisions (time, place, etc.), you need to broaden your team by adding your selected attendants—selected, perhaps, by using the process described above.

While each of these people will offer you input and opinion, ideally you should depend primarily on advice from your fiancé, both sets of parents, and your Maid of Honor and Best Man.

You may choose to believe that your committee of advisors is a participatory democracy, but here the majority does NOT rule. You and your fiancé must eventually decide what is best for your vision of the wedding. All final decisions are yours and your fiancé's alone!

And speaking of your fiancé . . .

It should be noted that you, the Bride, usually make most of the decisions. It may sound like a sexist cliché, but most Grooms tend to leave the majority of the decision-making to their fiancés. It isn't that they don't care, but rather that most Grooms recognize that the day is not about them—it's all about you! Therefore, they want you to make the majority of relevant decisions so that you have your perfect day. (Now, it's just possible that this may also be a defense mechanism, leaving them an out if things *don't* go as planned. "Hey, honey, *you* made the decision, not me!" Sneaky and cheeky rascals, those Grooms!)

However, *your* partner may be happy to help, adopt that "hands-off" attitude, or fall somewhere in between. Whatever his attitude, always ask his opinions and involve him—even if it means you drag him kicking and screaming into the process! This person is going to be your partner in life *for the rest of your life,* so involve him in the planning of the events that will make him so!

To show that you want his partnership and value his opinion, it is always best to be polite and ask him questions, even if you know he is reluctant to answer them. One possible format for these questions:

"What do *you* think? Is it okay for ______ to ______?"

Examples:

"What do you think? Is it okay for each of us to make personal vows?"

"What do you think? Is it okay for my niece, Lillie, to be the flower girl?"

By the way, when I was asked these kinds of questions by my fiancé, my stock answer was "If it's okay with you, it's okay with me." Although I wasn't overly concerned with the minutiae of the wedding planning, I was always happy that I was consulted about the plans. This will most likely be your partner's answer and attitude as well.

Regardless of the amount of participation your partner is willing to give, your fiancé will certainly have a say in all budget considerations, and many ask to be part of the selection of the reception menu, the cake flavor and decoration, the bar setup and the drinks to be served, and the entertainment. Beyond that, most Grooms defer to their partner's judgment.

CHOOSING THE RIGHT PEOPLE

The rules for choosing your Wedding Party . . . there are none! There is no generic checklist. Each Wedding Party is as unique as the Bride and Groom themselves; unique to them, their vision for the wedding, and their circumstance and situation.

This book is titled a guide because it will lead you in determining how best to choose and use the people right for you and your image of the wedding.

Are there general concepts? Certainly, and that's what this chapter is all about. Are there wedding traditions? Most assuredly; however, that doesn't mean that *you* have to follow them. As I keep reminding you, this is *your* wedding and you can pretty much do as you please.

General Considerations

Now that you are familiar with a basic decision-making process, you need to consider a number of things when actually selecting members for your Wedding Party. Amongst them are the following:

Budget and Finances—Expenses are important to consider when making your selection of members for your Wedding Party. For them, it includes the cost of formalwear (gowns and tuxedos), footwear, hair and makeup, accessories, etc. and may include the cost of travel and lodging. For you and your fiancé (and, most likely one or both sets of your parents) it may include the cost of a larger reception venue, additional catering, more flowers, accessories, the cost of thank you gifts, etc.—in addition to the cost of their "plus ones" at the reception, if you are allowing plus ones at your reception. The bottom line is: the more members of the Wedding Party, the greater the expense for all concerned.

Venue—As mentioned, the larger the Wedding Party, the larger the venue for both the *rehearsal* dinner and the reception, and, perhaps, even the ceremony site. Perhaps the venue(s) you prefer can't handle additional guests, hasn't enough parking, etc.

Note: If you *must* have a particular venue and it cannot accommodate everyone, it is better to pare the guest list than to limit the members of your Wedding Party.

Remember, the members of the Wedding Party are those people that you deem *essential* to the success of your wedding.

<u>Family and Religion</u>—If you have, or are marrying into, a large family, you may feel obligated to have both additional Bridesmaids and Groomsmen. Moreover, if you extend the definition of "family" to include you and your partner's close friends, the number of attendants may grow even larger. There could also be family or religious traditions requiring that you have a certain number of attendants. Moreover, if yours is an interfaith marriage, there may be certain customs and rituals that could require changes to your Wedding Party plans.

While family dynamics, such as divorce, can play a role in your particular wedding, it is beyond the scope of this book to help you. Divorce can make planning a wedding tricky, so it is best to have thought about and decided on the roles of biological and stepparents in consultation with them long before the ceremony.

Note: Some ideas I have observed at several weddings where this was a consideration: you may wish to have your biological parents walk the aisle together, even though one or both have remarried; their current spouses are already seated in the family pews. Or, you may want to have your biological parents walk together followed by your stepparents. You might also consider having your mom walk the aisle just a few steps ahead of your stepmom, and having both your dad and stepdad escort you to the altar. Your biological dad then gives you a kiss and sits down, while your stepdad "gives you away," or vice-versa.

Remember too, your parents have *roles* in both the wedding and the reception, with duties and responsibilities at each event. If a parent cannot perform these due to age, infirmity, distance, divorce, or decease, then you may need to choose someone(s) else must perform them. This person (or persons) may act as a proxy for the missing parent or depending on the circumstance, an actual replacement for them. If that person is a proxy, and the parent is able, the parent may then "walk the wedding" and whoever performed the duties is a special honored guest (seated with the family at the wedding, invited to the rehearsal dinner, the reception, and all other activities, etc.) If that person is replacing the parent, he or she has assumed most or all the duties of the parent and should be accorded full honors.

While the number of Bridesmaids and Groomsmen chosen is ultimately up to you and your partner, depending on your needs, many wedding planners suggest that you consider the attendants proportional to the total number of guests. In other words, a small wedding means a small number of attendants and a large wedding a greater number of attendants. The ratio is roughly one attendant for every thirty to fifty guests for an average wedding—although, in my experience, there is no such thing as an average wedding!

Finally, you must understand that the successes of your wedding events (rehearsal, ceremony, and reception) are often dependent on not just the number of your attendants, but the *quality* of your attendants. Choose wisely!

. . .

It is a good idea to have a general concept of what you want for your wedding ceremony and reception (inspiration and theme), an idea of the venue and the décor, food, entertainment, etc. *before* you consider choosing attendants. This is important because it is your responsibility to have an outline of a plan of action, a list of any DIY projects, an ideal guest list, some information on local vendors, etc. This way you can explain to your attendants the specifics of what you need them to do (perhaps help you choose options from among your lists) and to have their personal promise that they can do it. Because of this, you'll want the right person for the right job to make certain that your planning is carried out. At the very least, the people you select must have the maturity to understand what is expected of them and to be able to accomplish those expectations. To that end, it is important that they be team players who grasp the cliché of "team": "Together, Everyone Achieves More." Because of this, you need to choose the right people for your attendants.

You have already read about the bare bones decision-making process and seen an example of how it works. However, there are many things to consider when choosing the right people for your Wedding Party. Once you truly understand that *everyone* in the Wedding Party has a role in making your wedding a success (or failure!), you'll want to be certain that you have the right people in place.

. . .

Some Wedding Party roles are filled automatically (and often involuntarily)—parents of the Bride and Groom, for example—i.e. Father of the Bride, Mother of the Groom, etc. (although that can be a little messy if there are family dynamics, such as divorce, stepparents, family squabbles, etc). As to the other members of the Wedding Party, you and your partner will each choose your own attendants.

Since you ask these people to volunteer, they must be carefully chosen by the both of you to avoid both your and their embarrassment.

Don't offer a position to someone out of obligation, family relationship, or friendship. It will be difficult, but you must temper your emotion with practicality when choosing people for your Wedding Party. A favorite cousin or best friend may seem an obvious choice, but if they live three states over and can only make it the day before the ceremony, they are not a practical choice.

The people you choose will become your personal attendants (Bridesmaids and Groomsmen), and they need to be able to get along well with each other and to follow the lead of whoever you choose from amongst them to be the Chief Bridesmaid (Maid/Matron of Honor) and Chief Groomsman (Best Man). You don't want anyone who could give a headache to an aspirin!

Therefore, you'll want attendants who:

+ <u>Want to be in the wedding</u> and are not reluctant to be;

+ <u>Appreciate the honor</u> of being chosen;

+ <u>Are supportive of your marriage</u>, and of both you and your partner;

+ <u>Are aware of and understand the many things you expect from them</u>;

+ <u>Are dependable, reliable, and responsible</u>—mature enough to fulfill their duties;

+ <u>Are able to work well with others</u>—are team players and not lone wolves;

+ <u>Can accept direction and leadership</u>

In addition to choosing your attendants, and depending on your plans for the ceremony, you may also need to choose others as *assistants*—not attendants—and these might include a flower girl, ring bearer, page, etc.

The key word here is "choosing." You and your partner will make the final choices. And it is both of your prerogative and obligation to make the hard choices. Indeed, it is your obligation to each other to "cuss and discuss" whom you will choose. Be as diplomatic as you can, but be firm in your decision.

I keep repeating this because I cannot emphasize this enough: It is *your* wedding and you won't have the wedding you want without getting the help you need!

Choosing Amongst Family and Friends

It isn't easy choosing from amongst family and friends for your Wedding Party. Not all family members may be your friends and some friends may be closer to you than some family members may. Trust me; it ain't easy making your choice! The following are a few things to consider that may help you when making your selections.

Do _not_ feel obligated to include recommendations from parents, siblings or friends when making your decision, unless you agree with their suggestion. You can be certain that their recommendations will be well-meaning, but do you really want the cousin from out of state whom you barely know to be an attendant? Chances are that you love your relative, but is that particular cousin _really_ a best friend? And, speaking of friends, most people have several friends, but who amongst them is your _closest_ friend? If choosing amongst friends give special consideration to the ones that you have been friends with for some time and with whom you will remain friends with for years to come. However, do not choose attendants should as a "reward" for closeness or friendship.

Also, just because you were a Bridesmaid (or your fiancé a Groomsman) at someone else's wedding, that doesn't mean that you are obligated to choose them to be a member of _your_ wedding—you do NOT have to return the favor.

And don't allow yourself to be swayed by friends or family who walk right up to you and ask to be a Bridesmaid or Groomsmen. The fact that they asked you without waiting to *be* asked is an automatic disqualification, as it shows that they lack several essential qualities for an attendant.

Remember: Invite anyone you want to the wedding—but be careful whom you choose as your personal attendants!

Make the decisions yourself, or with the help of your partner (although they may not know some of the people you've selected) and/or ONE chosen advisor. That advisor might be a parent (most usually your mom) or your Maid of Honor/Best Man if you have already chosen them. Sometimes, though, it's best to have an objective third party help you. However, this person will need to know both you and the people you have selected pretty well—so perhaps they might be a friend, classmate, fellow worker, or clergy. In addition, when it comes to advice, it is usually true that experience trumps age. So, advice from a recently married friend about wedding planning is often more relevant than advice from your well-meaning grandmother. (Sorry, Grams!) The point is, it is okay to get advice and another's opinions, but the final decision must always be your own.

It's always best to choose more people than you really need. For instance, if you want three attendants, choose five people. Then begin to rank them as choices—first, second, etc. as you read in the chapter on decision-making. Allow yourself options. It's always possible that the person you ask will decline for one reason or another, so this way you'll have another person ready to ask.

And don't forget that <u>you are welcome to choose *your partner's* brother or sister</u> to be a Bridesmaid or Grooms-man (or even Maid of Honor or Best Man). After all, they are about to become family! As long as they are capable, feel free to ask. But, as with your own siblings, you are under no obligation to do so.

As mentioned, <u>the people you select should have an *active* role in your life</u>. They should be persons you are close to and see often. There will be a lot of work to do and everyone needs to get along well and be comfortable with each other—but especially with you AND your partner. They should be people who are a part of your life *now* and will continue to be a part of your life *after* the wedding.

<u>Never surprise your choice with your announcement.</u> Let them know that you are considering them and explain what you need them to do. They will be flattered by your consideration and forewarned as to what you expect from them.

<u>If possible, ALWAYS ask the person you choose *in person.*</u> If you can't because they live elsewhere, then telephone them and ask. The phone is much more personal than a letter, but write one if you have to. NEVER ask them by email or text message!

<u>Before asking someone, always consider his or her circumstances.</u> Knowing the person as you should, you must

consider their personal circumstances. Unless you are fairly certain that they will say "yes," don't ask them. You don't want to embarrass them or yourself. Some things about them you must consider (and reasons they may decline) include:

They live a considerable distance away;

They have problems traveling;

They have their own or a family members health considerations to take into account;

They have job, education, or family commitments (such as young children);

The event timing is off (wrong date, time of year, etc.) for them (they already used up their vacation time, it's the busy time of year at work, they can't take the kids out of school, etc.);

They don't have the finances need to travel, lodge, rent/buy attire, etc.

Again, if this person is a close friend, you should know them well enough to be able to take the above into account.

When you finally do ask the person to be a part of your wedding, do not feel slighted if they thank you but decline. Remember that being an attendant means an investment in time and money for the person you select, and they simply may not be able to make those commitments. This is especially true of those who may have to travel from elsewhere and bear the additional expense of travel, accommodation, formalwear purchase/rental, etc. Also, it is possible that they may say "yes" at first and then change their mind once you explain what you expect from them. They might have considered their position merely ceremonial and not have expected the work involved. Most likely, though, they realize that they simply won't have the time to devote to the position of attendant. (It's even possible that they do not consider themselves to be as close to you as you feel you are to them. This is sometimes the case with "casual friends" from school or work.)

If someone you ask does decline your invitation, <u>DO NOT try and "guilt" them into accepting</u>. If you do and they reluctantly accept, their efforts will probably be half-hearted at best and will certainly strain (and possibly end) whatever relationship you have with them. If you ask them and they say "no," thank them for having considered it, wish them well, and move on to your next choice. <u>Do not hold their "no" against them</u>. Be understanding and gracious. Besides, most likely they are truly and sincerely flattered that you asked, honestly wish they could be an attendant, and feel bad that they had to decline.

However, <u>if you are certain that they WILL decline</u>, but they are a close relative or friend, you can always write them a note letting them know that you considered them, but knew better than to ask. Such a note is usually received warmly by the recipient and goes a long way in showing your consideration for them and their circumstances. A quick note can save a friendship and keep peace in the family.

Rather than struggling over limiting your selection to a chosen few, <u>consider having *two* groups of attendants</u>. The first group consists of your <u>personal attendants</u>—those who will be Bridesmaids/Groomsmen and stand with you during the ceremony, and the other group fulfilling the role of the ushers and helpers who attend to the guests. They are your "<u>honorary attendants,</u>" and may be teen or adult ushers, and Junior Bridesmaids/Groomsmen who, to keep costs down, do not have to dress formally but are identified by a boutonniere or corsage and receive an inexpensive gift for their assistance. Their position is primarily ceremonial, with limited duties to perform.

Choosing a Chief Bridesmaid and Chief Groomsman

In the previous chapter, I offered an example of the decision-making process for choosing a Maid of Honor and/or Best Man. The following are a few of the many things you must consider when making this important decision.

After all, though you are the Chairman of the Board of "My Wedding, Inc.", you need to select a team leader from amongst your Bridesmaids (as your fiancé needs to do from his Groomsmen). These "chiefs" (your Maid of Honor and Best Man) <u>must</u> be chosen because of their unique qualifications and aptitude for the duties and responsibilities required by you and not because of family relationship or friendship. They will hold special positions with special responsibilities and are not just a "better Bridesmaid" or a "glorified Groomsman."

When choosing your "chiefs" you must remember that they need to be someone with these characteristics:
<u>open friendliness,</u>
<u>leadership ability,</u>

<u>maturity</u>—so that they can handle the duties and responsibilities you've planned for them.

Remember too, that since they will be witnesses to the ceremony as well as signing the marriage certificate, and/or other legal documents, they need to be at least 18 years old.

Choosing a Chief Bridesmaid/Groomsman often means having to choose between best friends (as today people often have several "besties") or between a sibling and a best friend, both of whom you consider close to you and who have each played a vital role in your life.

If you have a tough time deciding between two *equally qualified* people for Maid of Honor/Best Man, remember this rule: <u>family ALWAYS trumps friends</u>! It's sister over best friend and brother over a best friend. That is, unless it's okay with your sibling to choose your friend and that sometimes happens. Or if your sibling says they simply can't perform all the duties expected of them. If that is the case, choose your oldest and closest best friend. After all, your sister or brother can still be an attendant, just not the *Chief* Bridesmaid/Groomsman.

A side note: when choosing a sibling from amongst several sisters or brothers, traditionally you choose the sibling closest in age to you. Moreover, these Chiefs have logistical and other duties to perform, so be certain that you choose someone mature enough and capable of fulfilling the responsibilities of the position.

Another key to choosing these special attendants is to remember that this is *your* wedding and you want what you want: <u>It's okay to have a "tradition be damned" attitude</u>!

For example, <u>it's alright to have *two* Maids of Honor and/or *two* Best Men</u> (that certainly makes decision making a little easier and might allow you to have an underage sibling in the position). Also, it's more than okay to have a *male* Bridesmaid and a *female* Groomsman. Likewise, it's okay to have a Maid of Honor or Best Man of the opposite sex—a "Man of Honor" and a "Best Woman." I have attended a wedding where the Groom's best friend was his sister and so he made her his "Best Man."

It is important to note, however, that whomever you choose to fill the role takes on the duties of that role. So, for example, a "Best Woman" would still be in charge of the Groomsmen, organize the bachelor party, etc. Because of this, if the person you choose is reluctant to fulfill some of those duties, then delegate those to another attendant. Perhaps you might make that person an "honorary Chief," and if they are doing many duties, allow them to stand with you and your chosen Chief during the ceremony. Why not? As I said, it's okay to have two Best Men or Maids of Honor.

Remember, too, that the Best Man <u>*always*</u> gives a speech at the rehearsal and reception, and the Maid of Honor <u>*usually*</u> does, you should choose someone comfortable with doing so. If the person you really want to have in that position isn't a good speaker, just ask them to make a brief toast instead of a formal speech. One of the other books in The Wedding Series, *Your Wedding Speech Made Easy: The "How-to" Guide for the Father of the Bride, the Best Man...and Everyone Else!* might be a good gift to give them.

One caveat to all of the above: Understand that <u>there could be egos crushed by your decision</u> of a Maid of

Honor/Best Man. Make certain that the people you have chosen for your attendants are mature enough to handle this.

If you don't think someone may be emotionally mature enough or have a fragile ego, then select someone else for an attendant. There is no reason to choose someone who constantly wonders, "Why is ___ here?" and "Why wasn't *I* chosen as the Chief Bridesmaid/Groomsman?" It's probable that such an attitude will result in lackluster performance from them, and you cannot afford to have your wedding undermined by petty jealousies among your attendants. You MUST have a cohesive team working toward your goal of a perfect wedding! Eliminate any "drama queens (or kings)" during your selection process.

Lastly, please remember that when it comes to selecting a Maid of Honor or Best Man: <u>The person you love to party with may *not* be the person you want in charge of the people working on your wedding events</u>. Just sayin'.

Considering all of the above, you can now understand why it is so important to create a team for its *synergy*—that is, its whole is greater than the sum of its parts. Individuals and their contributions to your team add up to more than those individual contributions; namely, you're getting the wedding you want!

USING THE RIGHT PEOPLE

Now that you have your "chosen few," what do you do with them?

Teamwork—How to get your team to work

Meetings

You cannot have an effective team working together if they aren't together in the first place. Obviously, they all need to "be on the same page" as to their duties, but first they need to be physically together.

Chances are that not everyone on your team knows everyone else. So hold a Wedding Party initial meet-and-greet. You and your Bridesmaids could have your own get-together, while your fiancé meets with his Groomsmen, but I recommend your hosting a joint get-together, introducing everybody to everyone else.

However, you choose to do it, you're doing it to get them comfortable with each other and with the agenda you have for them. However, though you will certainly have other meetings with some or all of your team going forward, remember to make this all-important first get-together a combination of both fun and business.

<u>When you do have future get-togethers, stays focused on the goals for your meeting</u>, but always keep everything informal. Just like meetings at work, provide snacks and drinks, and keep it "business casual."

And don't forget technology—today you can "meet online," hold a conference call, or simply phone/text an individual member of the Wedding Party to see how they are doing.

Leadership

It's not a bad idea to use a business as an example of how to use a Wedding Party effectively. After all, you are in the business of achieving your perfect wedding—"My Wedding, Inc." so to speak. Therefore, consider yourself, as I said before, the Chairperson of the Board. Your Mom an advisor (perhaps your Groom's mom as well), and your Maid of Honor (perhaps the Best Man, too) as your Company president(s) and second(s) in command. The other members of your Wedding Party are your employees.

Note: One caveat before we start, although we might consider most members of your Wedding Party as "employees" in our example, in reality, they are not. You are not paying them for their time and effort. Each person has his or her own life to lead. Lives with family, social, and job commitments. Understand that each person may not be able to give you his or her full attention to the wedding preparations. Accept that and be okay with it. Learn to manage both your team *and* your expectations.

Perhaps most importantly, DO NOT let this experience hurt your friendships. These people may be your temporary "employees," but they are your permanent friends!

First, understand that YOU are the head honcho, and your team will look to you for leadership, preparedness, responsiveness to their needs, and effective means of communications, both from you to them and from them to you. Understand what you need from them, and what they need from you. Prepare to be a leader. Make certain that you are ready for the role. Lead by example, get in and get dirty—roll up your proverbial sleeves. Always ask and suggest, don't dictate and demand. <u>Be a boss, not a "bridezilla."</u>

<u>To have an effective team, *you* need to know what you need *them* to do</u>. As I have said, you should already have an idea of what they need to do to prepare for your wedding and a rough timeline to accomplish each thing (your countdown timeline).

You must be plainspoken about your requirements. It is not their job to second-guess you or decide for you because if they do, it will ultimately lead to disappointment. It is your job to let everyone know what *you* want and need from them.

Explain your wedding theme. (See the next chapter.)

Perhaps you have already decided on some of the details or perhaps you need your team to brainstorm some helpful ideas. Whatever theme you've chosen, make certain that now and going forward, you make your objectives clear and that everyone completely understands their tasks so that you achieve your goals.

Since you have created a team, it is important for you to understand that the trite definition of "team" as an acronym is a truism: team = Together Everyone Achieves More. Synergy, remember? Appreciate the differences and individual skills that each person you choose brings to your team. No two people will be alike, so value the fact that each one will contribute to the best of their ability in differing and unique ways.

Make certain that you give tasks to the person(s) best able to accomplish them. Again, appreciate each person's unique set of skills. If you have no one with the particular set of skills needed, use a "volunteer." (See the chapter, *"Volunteer" Attendants*.)

Some Brides are relatively unreachable and choose to be *apart from* their team, rather than *be a part of it*. Don't you be like "some Brides!" Stay involved. Lead through active participation. Always be supportive, enthusiastic, and positive. <u>Show your team members that you value them by working with them.</u>

As I have suggested, you should <u>hold team meetings when practical, but certainly stay in touch</u> by phone or text. Ask them how they are doing, both personally and with whatever task they have been assigned. Your team member is always happy to hear from "the boss."

Ideally, everyone starts with incredible enthusiasm and every initial task is accomplished in full and on time. Then, Reality gets a hint of what's going on and says, "Ain't gonna happen."

As you can imagine, not everything will go as planned. There will be setbacks, miscommunications, and outright failures. Expect them. Be psychologically prepared for them. Keep yourself and your team upbeat and positive. Learn from your problems and work around and through them. You are the team leader—so lead!

(See the chart at the end of this chapter to better understand standard reporting relationships.)

Delegation

Make certain that you are able to delegate work and that you don't micromanage—after all, that's why you have "supervisors"—your Mom(s) and your Maid of Honor. Remind your team that coordinators oversee them and they should initially address any questions and concerns to them, and not to you directly—you have enough to do!

By the time you assemble your Party, you most likely already have a venue for the ceremony chosen, especially if it is to be a religious ceremony. But, if you are like most Brides, once you have a preliminary guest list you <u>will need for them to help with research</u> into reception venues and vendors, as well as research on other things (such as printers for the invitations, online sources for décor, etc.). Those with computer skills and "telephone personality" are ideal for these tasks.

If you already have a venue for both the ceremony and the reception, and your vendors were chosen, your Party will have only several basic duties to perform.

These traditional duties are outlined in the following chapters but remember—chances are that you will put your personal spin on these basic duties, *plus* add your own ideas and needs to make your unique vision of your wedding a reality. When it comes to weddings, nothing is carved in stone, so cherry-pick, modify, add, do whatever you want! But <u>it is *your* duty to let each team member know what they have to do</u>. And those <u>duties will evolve and change over time</u> as you proceed with your preparations. Things that seemed of great importance may not actually be that important, while minor details might suddenly loom large.

Communication

Make your team aware that since they will need to be able to help you make decisions, that they can always speak up, and that you value their opinion and input. <u>Involve them. Make them feel that both they and their opinions matter to you</u>. But understand that not every idea, thought, or opinion will have merit. However, listen to what is said, consider it, and then, if need be, provide constructive criticism. Don't use destructive criticism and be dismissive outright, because doing so belittles you and your team member, and may force them to keep their opinions to themselves—even when they have a great idea! So, <u>keep communications open</u>.

You must understand that not everyone will agree with your decisions. While well-meaning advice and suggestions about your decisions are always welcomed, you can expect that there will also be *un*welcomed criticism as well, and that's normal for any group. Politely listen, but remember, it's *your* wedding, not theirs! Do what you must to make it right for you and your fiancé!

(See the chart at the end of this chapter to better understand standard communication flow.)

Conflict/Resolution

Because of each team members individuality, there will probably be disagreements amongst your team at some point—and that's okay. But arguments . . . not so much. Differences of opinion are to be expected and can often lead to something good, as in a brainstorming session. These sparks can be beneficial if you remember that there can be no fire without friction.

<u>While everyone is there for the common cause of helping you get the wedding you want, that doesn't mean that everything will go smoothly</u>. So be prepared!

Even though you have already weeded out the divas and showboats when you were first choosing your team, there will always be some minor conflicts when people work together. <u>You need to understand that personalities clash, work ethics may differ amongst your team, some people are better at certain tasks than others are, and so on</u>. Unfortunately, you won't really know any of this until you all begin to work together. I mention it now to make you aware that these things will most likely occur. How you resolve these issues will depend, in large part, on your personality and your willingness to involve yourself in the process. So be personable and understanding, but authoritative.

Always <u>try to be consistent and show no favoritism</u> or preference for family over friend or friend over new acquaintance. Be as fair as possible.

Let them know that should there be a problem or personality conflict, they can talk with you (this should be the only occasion that you encourage them to contact you directly) or your Maid of Honor. Make them understand that someone is always there for them to talk to and confide in. And if a task is too much for them, remind them that it is always okay to ask for help with the problem—whether it is a clash of character, the process, or the procedure for achieving their assigned task. However, <u>your job is not to hand-hold</u>, and if you need to, <u>it is certainly okay to change that persons task to something else and/or give it another team member to finish</u>. As I said, appreciate each person's abilities and support their individual initiative, but recognize their limitations as well.

• • •

As someone with supreme insight and wisdom once wrote:

44

*"The only true failure is failing to learn
from the mistakes you make."*

Okay . . . it was me, in one of the other books in *The Wedding Series*. Perhaps it isn't an original thought, but it is appropriate. The sentiment may be ancient but the wisdom is timeless.

If you follow the above, both you and your team should be more productive in helping you create the wedding you've dreamed of. Thus, you'll profit from the tasks being accomplished both on time and within your budget. And who could ask more from *any* business!

. . .

Typical Wedding Party Communications/Leadership Chart*
(Remember: Communication travels both ways.)

Bride/Groom

‖

Maid of Honor/Best Man ≡ Mother of the Bride/Groom

‖

Task Leaders

‖

Bridesmaids/Groomsmen/Others

*It should be noted that the Fathers of the Bride and Groom are conspicuously absent from the chart. This is because, in my experience, most Dads defer from speaking for their daughter or son. Their usual answer to any question put to them by a Bridesmaid or Groomsman is something like, "Oh I don't want to speak for my (daughter/son). It's best to ask my wife (or the Maid of Honor or Best Man)." Of course, your father and your Groom's father might be more participatory. Maybe, maybe not.

THE BRIDE AND GROOM'S JOINT DUTIES

This is only a partial list of the things you and your fiancé need to think about. Again, this book is not a wedding planner, but a supplement to help you with just one aspect of your wedding planning—choosing and using the members of your Wedding Party. I am certain that you'll receive input from both sets of parents, other family members, and your closest friends, whether you want it or not. As most of it will be well-meaning, and, perhaps, even helpful, always consider and take under advisement what is said. But understand that the decisions you both make must be your own. Cussed, discussed, compromised (maybe) but always arrived at jointly.

Brides, please note: For some of the joint duties, it might seem that your Groom is disinterested and prefers that "you choose" and will then just sign off on it. As I wrote before, Do NOT let this happen! Both of you MUST take an active role in the planning or trouble can occur later on. Some Grooms will want an active role in the wedding planning and have ideas of their own. However, remember that most Grooms understand that the wedding day will be focused on you, the Bride, and so they most likely simply want you to plan the "perfect day" as you see it, and are more than willing to let you have the wedding you want.

However, if you must, drag him kicking and screaming into the wedding planning process (but not to the altar, though—that would really make for a rocky start to your marriage!).

．　．　．

Again, understanding that this book is *not* intended to be a complete wedding planner, the following are *some* of the things that you might consider jointly.

—By the way, I assume that you already have the marriage license!

<u>Plan your wedding events budget.</u>

This includes the pre-wedding events, the wedding, the reception, and the honeymoon. Though traditionally the Father of the Groom pays for the rehearsal dinner and the Father of the Bride pays for both the wedding and the reception (the Groom almost always pay for the honeymoon), today the wedding events are most often funded jointly by both families of The Couple, and with The Couple contributing as well. Indeed, many Brides and Grooms now pay the majority of the expenses. However, you split up the finances, talk with both sets of parents and make it a family decision.

<u>Decide on the Wedding Events you both want:</u>

Engagement party;
Bride's attendants' initial get-together;
Grooms attendants' initial get-together (maybe hold the events together?);
Bridal shower;
Bachelor and bachelorette parties (if wanted);
"Thank-You" party/parties for juniors, "volunteer" attendants, etc.;
Rehearsal;
Rehearsal dinner;
PLUS the (at least bi-weekly) get together with your attendants to work on projects or to coordinate wedding-related activities;

And, oh yeah,
The Wedding Ceremony and
The Reception!

<u>Decide on a style and/or theme for your wedding</u>.

<u>Traditional or non-traditional</u> ("church" wedding or one at the beach);

<u>Formal or informal</u> (both in attitude towards the events, and the attire—suits and formalwear for guests, business casual, or tropical print shirts and shorts?);

<u>The Reception</u> (sit-down dinner at a country club, outdoor BBQ, catering by your family members, or a private room at your favorite restaurant?), live music or a DJ ?; etc.

<u>What about a theme wedding</u> based on: a favorite movie or television show (we've all seen *Star Trek* and *Star Wars* weddings, even *Game of Thrones*-themed weddings [the Red Wedding, not so much!]); a favorite era (a Roaring Twenties/Gatsby-theme, etc.); your favorite color predominating in various hues at the wedding and reception; etc.

.   .   .

Note: You might want to consider doing the following *after* you have selected your Wedding Party so that you receive input and help from them.

<u>Select a date</u> (may change once a decision has been made on the venue)

<u>Time of year</u> ("June" bride, an autumn, mid-summer wedding?)

<u>Day of the week</u> (traditional Fri/Sat/Sun wedding? What about a Tuesday night?)

<u>Time of day</u> (sunrise at the beach, traditional evening ceremony, etc.)

<u>Research</u> on:

<u>Venues</u> (wedding ceremony and reception);

<u>Vendors</u>: including the caterer, florist, baker, photographer and/or videographer, musicians/DJ, etc.

<u>Research, choose and shop for the wedding attire</u> (and thank you gifts)

For yourselves and your potential attendants; deciding on colors and styles; price range/rental charges, etc.

<u>The Wedding Ceremony</u>

Meet with the officiant to discuss details of the wedding—venue, date, procedure, rites, plus any pre-marriage counseling requirements*, etc.

<u>Begin Considering the General Members of the Wedding Party</u>

You will each individually list and consider your personal attendants (Bridesmaids and Groomsmen), but you must jointly decide on ancillary assistants for the ceremony, if needed, such as a ring bearer, flower girl, any juniors and honorary attendants, etc.

<u>Consider the miscellany</u>

Discuss and plan for the roles of both natural and stepparents, and natural and stepchildren (if needed);

Create a guest list (and no, you DO NOT need to invite everyone suggested to you!);

Create and/or order invitations, maps/directions to the wedding and reception sites;

Understand your needs as newlyweds and register at stores and/or websites appropriate for those needs;

Set up a wedding website (optional, but very handy for communication, especially for those from out of your area plus you can announce any changes to your plans instantly!);

Decide on some gift ideas for both of your parents, the Maid of Honor, Best Man,

Bridesmaids, Groomsmen, Junior Bridesmaids and Junior Groomsmen.

Plan DIY projects (and there are always
some)—centerpieces, favors, decorations,
etc.

Once the above are pretty much decided on by you and
your fiancé, and with input (wanted or not) from both your
families, you will have a general idea of what needs to be
done to make your wedding happen the way you want it
to.

*Whether or not you choose to or are required to attend
pre-marriage counseling, this book may be helpful,

*Questions for Couples: What to Ask Before You Say "I Do": A
Primer for Planning Your Future Together and A Guide to What to
Expect From Premarital Counseling*

THE BRIDE'S DUTIES

Note: This is obviously NOT a complete list of the Bride's duties, in fact, it barely scratches the surface! Your actual duties would vary with the decisions you've made concerning the date, time, place of the wedding, number of guests, your personal preferences for décor, color choices etc. Also, although these are some of the traditional duties of the Bride, many of today's couples share the decision-making, planning, and payments for things like the honeymoon, wedding bands, etc. thus making several of these joint decisions instead of yours alone.

<u>Your expenses</u>

Purchase your Grooms wedding ring and arrange for any engraving. (He already gave you the engagement ring, hasn't he?)

Purchase gifts for your Groom, and your Maid of Honor and Bridesmaids (Juniors, too). Also, purchase gifts for both sets of parents, though The Couple often does this jointly.

General Duties

Prior to the Wedding

+ Choose your Bridesmaids and select a Maid of Honor from amongst them.
  (After all, that's why you bought this book!)

+ Host a luncheon for your Bridesmaids as both a meet-and-greet and to discuss their duties, etc.

+ Decide on a schedule of regular team meetings with all or some of your Wedding Party to make certain you are on track to accomplish your goals, do DIY projects, address and mail invitations and follow-ups, etc.

+ With the Maid of Honor and/or your mother (perhaps the Groom's mother, too):

  Set up and maintain the Wedding Binder—the central place for all the information regarding vendors, venues, costs, checklists, names, addresses, and phone numbers, etc.

+ Research, shop for and select your wedding gown and accessories.

+ Select your day-of jewelry.

+ Decide on your make-up, hairstyle, mani-pedi, and who will do them.

+ Research and select the style, color, etc. of your Bridesmaids' dresses.

+ Be nice to your Bridesmaids and choose a dress they can wear *after* your wedding. They pay for their gowns, so make it something semi-formal that can be worn for eveningwear. No wild styles or colors! Also, it is best to get their input. After all, even though this is *your* wedding, your Bridesmaids are paying for their dresses and they will become a permanent part of their wardrobe. And don' forget, it may be possible to rent Bridesmaids gowns just as Groomsmen rent their tuxedos!

+ Arrange dates and times for fittings for yourself and your Bridesmaids.

+ Also, decide on the hair and makeup styles for the Bridesmaids, as well as suggested jewelry and accessories.

+ Help consult on and choose the Mothers of the Bride and Groom dresses with each woman.

+ Obtain any necessary documents needed for the honeymoon (passport, visas, etc.)

+ Pack for the honeymoon.

+ If you are changing your name, make arrangements for and complete any paperwork necessary to change the name on your driver's license, credit cards, bank accounts, etc. as well as update your address (if needed) for these and such mundane things as magazine subscriptions, etc.

+ Write personal vows for the wedding ceremony (if so doing)*

+ Write a speech for the reception*

The Day of the Wedding

Prior to the ceremony

+ The Bride traditionally arrives with his parents and/or the Maid of Honor.

+ Make sure you have the Groom's ring—it's best to give it to your Maid of Honor for safekeeping.

During the Ceremony (depending on tradition)

+ Your father or whomever you've designated traditionally escorts you down the aisle.

+ You, of course, look gorgeous!

+ You carry your beautiful bridal bouquet.

+ During the ceremony, you hand the bouquet to her Maid of Honor to hold until the end of the ceremony.

After the Ceremony

+ You and the Groom pose for any formal photographs and informal family photos.

+ You both leave late to allow the guests to arrive at the reception before you. After all, you want to make a grand entrance, don't you?

At the Reception

+ You and the Groom may stand in a formal reception line or simply make an entrance once the guests have arrived.

+ You and the Groom sit at the table of honor, either by yourselves or with the Best Man and Maid of Honor.

+ Today, you may make a speech thanking everyone for attending, welcoming your new in-laws, thanking your Maid of Honor and Bridesmaids, and making a tribute to your Groom, ending with a toast to him.*

+ If there is a formal dance, you'll dance with your Groom, your father, and the Grooms father.

+ You and the Groom will mingle with the guests, often visiting each guest table offering personal thank-yous and a chance for informal photographs.

+ You'll probably dance with family and friends.

+ At some point during the reception, you and the Groom may change clothes and exit for the honeymoon. The exit is a formal affair and the guests often throw confetti, blow bubbles, etc. (no one today throws rice!) to wish you well. Your departure also often relieves guests of the formality of the reception and allows for a freer party! So, enjoy your reception but when you leave—leave! Let "the real party" begin.

The Tao of the Vow: The Path to YOUR Perfect Vows – How to Write and Deliver YOUR Wedding Vows

And

YOUR Wedding Speech Made Easy: The "How-to" Guide for The Couple (Writing and Delivering YOUR Perfect Wedding Speech)

THE GROOM'S DUTIES

Note: This is obviously NOT a complete list of your fiancé's duties, as that would vary with the decisions you've made concerning the date, time, place of the wedding, number of guests, etc. Also, although these are some of the traditional duties of the Groom, you may—like many of today's couples—share the decision-making, planning, and payments for things like the honeymoon, wedding bands, etc. thus making these decisions joint decisions.

<u>His expenses</u>

He plans and pays for the honeymoon.

He makes all reservations for destination (hotel, resort, etc.) and travel plans (purchase tickets, arrange transportation to and from air/seaport, etc.), secures any necessary travel documents (such as passports and visas), get travelers checks and/or verifies the charge cards are accepted wherever you are going, etcetera.

He packs for the honeymoon.

He purchases the Bride's wedding ring and arranges for any engraving. (He already gave you the engagement ring, didn't he?)

He purchases gifts for his Bride, the Best Man, and Groomsmen (Juniors, too). He also purchases gifts for both sets of parents, though The Couple often does this jointly.

He makes arrangements for his and your day-of transportation to both the wedding and reception sites; and pays for the driver, limo rental, etc., if necessary.

He also <u>pays for the following</u>:

The bridal bouquet;

The corsages and boutonnieres for the Wedding Party;

The officiates fees (though this actually given to the officiate by the Best Man);

The fee for any additional ushers, if any, hired as wedding staff;

And, often, the musical entertainment (DJ, musicians, etc.)

General Duties

Prior to the Wedding

+ He must select his Groomsmen and choose a Best Man from amongst them.

+ He will cover the duties and responsibilities of a Best Man with the person he has chosen, and the responsibilities of the Groomsmen with him also, so that he and the Best Man can cover these with them when…

+ He hosts a luncheon for his Groomsmen as both a meet-and-greet and to discuss their duties, etc.

  Note: this is why it is so important that you share this book with him!

+ He will write personal vows for the wedding ceremony (if so doing)*

+ He will write speech for the reception*

<u>With his Best Man and/or his own father, he will</u>:

+ Research, plan and book hotel rooms or make other accommodations for out-of-town attendees.

+ Research and suggest local rental car services for out-of-town attendees, or arrange other transportation.

+ Research rentals and arrange for his Best Man's and Groomsmen attire.

+ Rent/purchase his own wedding attire and accessories.

+ Arrange dates and times for both his and their fittings.

+ Help his father (the traditional host of the event) plan and organize the rehearsal dinner, and notify the members of the Wedding Party as to its time and place.

+ If using his own car for the honeymoon, prepare it by getting the car washed and waxed, checking the tires, gas, oil, brakes, etc. And make certain that he has maps and/or GPS to get to the honeymoon location.

The Day of the Wedding

Prior to the ceremony

+ The Groom traditionally arrives with his parents and/or his Best Man.

+ He and his parents may see and greet the Parents of the Bride (though, traditionally, he will not greet or see the Bride herself).

+ He carries the marriage license and the wedding ring or gives them to the Best Man to carry for him.

During the Ceremony (depending on tradition)

+ He may walk the aisle in processional, followed by his Best Man and Groomsmen, who walk alone or escort the Bridesmaids.

Or

+ He stands at the altar with his Best Man and Groomsmen prior to the start of the ceremony.

After the Ceremony

+ He and you pose for any formal photographs and informal family photos.

+ You both leave the ceremony site late to allow the guests to arrive at the reception first.

At the Reception

+ He and you may stand in a formal reception line or simply make an entrance once the guests have arrived.

+ He and you sit at the table of honor, either by themselves or with the Best Man and Maid of Honor.

+ He traditionally makes a speech thanking everyone for attending, welcoming his new in-laws, thanking his Best Man and Groomsmen, and making a tribute to his beautiful Bride, ending with a toast to you.*

+ If there is a formal dance, he dances with you, his mother, and your mother.

+ He and you mingle with the guests, often visiting each guest table offering personal thank-yous and a chance for informal photographs.

+ He and you both usually dance with family and friends.

+ At some point during the reception, he and you may change clothes and exit for the honeymoon. The exit is a formal affair and the guests often throw confetti, blow bubbles, etc. to wish The Couple well (no one throws rice anymore!). The departure also often relieves guest of the formality of the reception and allows for a freer party.

The Tao of the Vow: The Path to YOUR Perfect Vows – How to Write and Deliver YOUR Wedding Vows
And
YOUR Wedding Speech Made Easy: The "How-to" Guide for The Couple (Writing and Delivering YOUR Perfect Wedding Speech)

THE MAID OF HONOR'S DUTIES

Also known as the Chief Bridesmaid, Bridesman (if a man is chosen), or by the gender-neutral term Chief Honor Attendant. If she is married, she is traditionally referred to as the Matron of Honor, but today many Brides prefer the term Maid of Honor regardless of her marital status.

She is the chief honor attendant for the Bride, acting as her dresser, personal attendant, and confidante. She supervises all Bridesmaids, making sure that they are aware of their duties and follows up to be certain those duties are performed. She coordinates all Bridesmaids' activities. As the Bride's main confidant, she is also the Bridesmaids "go to" for any questions, so that the bride-to-be is not disturbed, although this duty may be shared with the Mother of the Bride.

Though often the Bride's sister or best friend, whoever is chosen must be at least 18 years old, as she will be a witness to the wedding and will sign the marriage certificate.

She is the Chief Bridesmaid, as the Best Man is the Chief Groomsman. As such, she is their leader. Her position is equal to the Best Man and she, therefore, shares a place of honor as the third most important member of the Wedding Party after Bride and Groom.

Her expenses

She is expected to pay for her wedding attire (formalwear and shoes), any alterations, and accessories. She may also have to pay for her hair and makeup, though this is often paid for by the Bride as a gift to her and her fellow Bridesmaids.

If from out of town, she often pays for her travel and lodging, although the Bride usually arranges accommodations, often at a relatives or friends home.

She is expected to present only one small bridal shower gift and one small, personal wedding gift to you, her duties as Maid of Honor being her major present for The Couple. You usually present her with a small personal gift to show her your appreciation.

•   •   •

Note: if the Maid of Honor is from out of town, several of the following may change.

General Duties

Prior to the Wedding

+ She helps both the Bride and the Mother of the Bride set up and maintain the Wedding Binder—the central organizational place for all the information regarding vendors, venues, costs, checklists, names, addresses, and phone numbers, etc.

+ Once it is established, she works with the Mother of the Bride to make sure the wedding timeline is followed for all activities, deliveries, etc.

+ Unless there is a wedding planner, she may be asked (usually along with the Mother of the Bride) to be the contact for the caterers and other vendors.

+ She may accompany the Bride, Groom (and often the Mothers of The Couple) as they visit venues for the wedding and reception, as well as florists, bakers, caterers, etc. The Maid of Honor is expected to give her <u>honest</u> opinion of places, styles, colors, tastes, etc. IF you ask her for it—so don't be shocked if she disagrees with you!

+ She may help the Bride research and shop stores and/or online for apparel, footwear, décor, favors, etc.

+ Along with the Bride, she hosts a Bridesmaid's "get together" luncheon as a "meet and greet" to both introduce the Bridesmaids to each other and to discuss their role in making the wedding a success.

+ The Maid of Honor makes a list of the Bridesmaid's names, addresses and home telephone numbers for her use. She is responsible for informing all Bridesmaid's not only *what* is required of them, but also *when* it is required. She may also be asked by the Bride to convey additional information to them as the wedding plans progress.

+ She will also need the phone number of the Best Man to coordinate information and make certain that the wedding timeline is followed.

+ The Maid of Honor helps plan the bridal shower (often with input from Bride, the Mother of the Bride, and the Mother of the Groom) and acts as its primary host.

+ Along with the Bride's family members and the other Bridesmaids, she helps address and stuff envelopes for the invitations, make any

DIY wedding decorations and/or favors for the reception, etc.

+ She attends pre-wedding activities, such as the bridal shower, the rehearsal, rehearsal dinner, etc. and sees to it that all Bridesmaids attend as well, providing them with the date and times for these events and coordinating transportation, if necessary.

+ She works with her fellow Bridesmaids to plan, coordinate, and pay for a bachelorette party — dependent on the Bride's preferences.

+ She may help the Bride comparison shop for the wedding gown and the Bridesmaids' dresses. She often is asked for her input as to the choice of style.

+ She also organizes her own and the other Bridesmaids dress fittings.

+ Along with the other Bridesmaids, she helps spread the word about where The Couple is registered, and may even be asked by the Bride to suggest gifts.

+ She works with the Bride (and sometimes the Groom or Best Man) to help find lodging and transportation for any Bridesmaids from out of town.

+ She records (or designates another Bridesmaid to record) all gifts received at the various pre-wedding events, keeping this in a special notebook, titled "Gift's Log." She usually gives this to the Mother of the Bride to hold until The Couple returns from their honeymoon.

+ May be asked by the Bride to assist her (and usually the Bride's mother and the Mother of the Groom) in creating seating arrangements for the reception.

+ As the Bride's chief maid, she should create and keep a "'Day of' Emergency Kit," bringing it with her on the wedding day. [See the Appendices]

+ Knowing that she will be primarily with you on "the big day," she selects a Bridesmaid to supervise the others, as her attention will be focused on you—the Blushing Bride.

+ She works with you to plan what the Bridesmaids need to do at the ceremony so that she can cover this with them and the appointed supervisor.

+ She works with her fellow Bridesmaids to select and purchase a gift for the Bride.

The Day of the Wedding

Prior to the ceremony

+ She may accompany the Bride to the ceremony. If not, she arrives the same time as the Bride, both arriving several hours early for dressing, hair, and makeup and other preparations for the ceremony.

+ She acts as the Bride's maid, helping her dress, prep for the ceremony, etc.; she carries the "'Day of' Emergency Kit," just in case it is needed.

+ She supervises the supervisor she has chosen to verify (amongst other things): the Bridesmaids have all arrived at the, are wearing the correct dresses, have both their hair and makeup done, and have the correct bouquets. And informs them of any last minute changes to the plan and agenda.

+ She helps gather her fellow Bridesmaids for any formal photos before the ceremony.

+ She is responsible for the return of the Bride's personal items to the Bride's house or designated recipient (usually the Mother of the Bride).

+ She confirms with the Best Man that the officiant has arrived and is prepared for the ceremony.

+ She coordinates with the Best Man to verify that all paperwork and luggage needed for the honeymoon are ready.

+ She may ask a Bridesmaid to verify that all family members are wearing the appropriate corsages or boutonnieres.

+ She may also bring a change of clothes for the Bride to change into for the reception. Usually, the Bride will change clothes either during the reception to "dress down" for the festivities but more likely, will do so before leaving the reception to start the honeymoon.

During the Ceremony (depending on tradition)

+ As the last Bridesmaid in the processional, she walks the aisle just before the Bride. The Best Man may escort her, or she may walk out singly during the processional.

+ She usually carries the Groom's ring. (If there is a ring bearer, the rings carried are usually faux rings, the Maid of Honor holding the real ring.)

+ She adjusts the Bride's veil and train at the altar (if necessary)

+ At the altar, she stands on the Brides left and slightly behind her.

+ She holds the bridal bouquet during the exchange of vows.

+ She gives the Bride the Groom's ring for the exchange of rings.

+ She returns the bridal bouquet to the Bride after The Couple's "first kiss."

+ She is usually escorted by the Best Man during the recessional.

After the Ceremony

+ She acts as a witness to the signing of the marriage certificate by The Couple, and traditionally, she and the Best Man sign the marriage certificate as witnesses.

+ She helps gather her fellow Bridesmaids and they pose for any formal photos.

+ As soon as any post-ceremony photos (if any) are taken, she leaves the wedding site, often with one other Bridesmaid and/or the Mother of the Bride, and arrives at the reception site before the guests. There, she may be joined by the Mother of the Bride to verify all is in order for the reception: decorations in place, wedding favors and centerpieces are on the tables, etc.

At the Reception

+ It is important that the Maid of Honor is familiar with the reception venue and the setup as the Bride may ask her and the other Bridesmaids to help at the reception showing guests their seats, where to find the guest books, showing them to the gift table, directing them to the restrooms, etc.

+ If there is a reception line, she stands to the Groom's left. If not…

+ She may be announced and enters with the Best Man at the reception.

+ If there is a head table, she is seated to the Groom's left.

+ She often makes a short speech and toasts the Bride and Groom.*

+ At the reception, she stays near to the Bride, may help bundle her train and veil; makes sure that she eats and has something to drink; keeps tissues nearby for the occasional tears of joy, etc. (You may also ask her to accompany you to the restroom, as your bridal gown is probably unwieldy.)

+ She helps the Bride change during the reception to more casual "party worthy" clothes and shoes and certainly does so just before you, dear Bride, depart for your honeymoon.

+ If there is a formal dance—After the Groom's dance with his new Bride, his mother and mother-in-law, she will then dance with him. After this, she usually dances with the Best Man.

+ She and the Best Man may be asked to encourage dancing if there is no wedding coordinator (host).

+ Regardless, she and the other bridesmaids mingle with the other guests, encourage them to dance, and may dance with unaccompanied guests.

+ You may ask her to help the Best Man collect any gift envelopes from the guests.

+ She and the other Bridesmaids gather the single female guests for the bouquet toss and may ask the Best Man and Groomsmen to help, as well.

+ She helps the Best Man organize the newly-wed's departure (seeing to it that The Couples luggage is loaded in the car, etc.) and helps decorate the "getaway" car.

+ If not done by the Father of the Bride (the traditional host), she and the Best Man close the evening by thanking everyone for attending and wishing them farewell.

+ She may assign two Bridesmaids to assist the Groomsmen in personally thanking the guests for attending as they exit the reception.

After the Reception

+ She is responsible for keeping both the bridal gown and bouquet safe until the Bride returns from the honeymoon (a duty often shared with or done by the Mother of the Bride).

+ She may be asked to return the Bride's rented attire, or—if it was purchased—has it dry cleaned and returns it to the Bride upon her return from the honeymoon.

+ If the Bridesmaid's dresses were rentals, she contacts all Bridesmaids to return them to her and she is responsible for returning them to the rental store.

+ She usually receives a personal "thank you" gift from the Bride.

+ She will often be asked by the Bride (and/or the Mother of the Bride) to join her as they open the gifts received at the reception and to record who gifted what. She'll add that information to the Gift's Log that she had previously kept to assist The Couple when writing their thank you cards.

+ She may be asked to join the Father of the Bride's morning-after party if one is given.

*YOUR Wedding Speech Made Easy: The "How-to" Guide for the Father of the Bride, the Best Man . . . and Everyone Else!   (Writing and Delivering YOUR Perfect Wedding Speech)

THE BRIDESMAIDS

Also known by the gender-neutral term, Honor Attendants

Bridesmaids are your personal attendants. They are usually chosen from amongst your closest family and friends. They may be single or married, and can be any age, but are usually sixteen or older. Younger girls should be considered for Junior Bridesmaid.

Your Maid of Honor is chosen from the Bridesmaids and is their direct liaison with you. The other Bridesmaids follow the directions of this Chief Bridesmaid.

Although you may choose as many Bridesmaids as you wish, most Brides choose only a Maid of Honor and perhaps one or two Bridesmaids. This is often because of the expense involved, especially if those chosen have to attend from out of town. To fulfill all duties you can always have

"Volunteer" Attendants and Honorary and/or Junior Bridesmaids.

The primary duty of a bridesmaid is to help you by being a friend, help you stay positive, console and comfort you when things don't go as planned: in short, offer emotional support and be a cheerleader!

Their expenses

If they have traveled from out of town, they traditionally pay for their own transportation, car rental, and also lodging. They pay for the rental/purchase of their formalwear, any alterations, accessories, and shoes, plus the cost of hair and makeup. They pay their share of the expenses for the shower and/or bachelorette party, as well as a portion of the expense for the Bride's gift.

General Duties

Prior to the Wedding

+ They meet with you and the Maid of Honor to learn in detail what is expected of them and to divide some of the duties.

+ They exchange their names and phone numbers with each other, and especially the Maid of Honor, to expedite communication so that any last-minute changes in their particular duties can be relayed to them.

+ They will attend an informal meeting with you and Maid of Honor to discuss your choice of their gowns, preferred hairstyle, and accessories, times and places for hair and makeup (if using local salons), etc. If they have reservations about your choices, it's okay to "cuss and discuss." I am certain that any objections will be tactful and well-meaning. Although the wedding attire is your vision, it's always best to hear from those who have to actually wear it!

+ They work with the Maid of Honor on organizing the rental/purchase and fittings for their formal attire, and hair and makeup.

+ They run errands as needed (and there will be *lots* of errands!).

+ They assist in preparing the wedding invitations, addressing envelopes, etc.

+ They meet the Groomsmen, in particular, their escort with whom they will "walk the aisle."

+ They may be asked to help inform people and "spread the word" about your registry at various stores and online.

+ They may assist the Maid of Honor in keeping a register of gifts received prior to the wedding at the various pre-wedding events.

+ They may help perform DIY and small arts and crafts projects like creating small bouquets, ribbons, and other decorations for the wedding venue and reception; they may be asked to create wedding favors for the guests at the reception, etc. In this, the Groomsmen may assist them.

+ They may assist with projects, such as creating a wedding program, creating maps to the reception, etc.

+ They may be asked to help decorate both the wedding and reception venues; often with help from the Groomsmen.

+ They help the Maid of Honor plan, organize, and pay for the shower/bachelorette party.

+ They attend that and any other parties—engagement, rehearsal, and reception.

+ Near the day of the ceremony, the Maid of Honor will select one of them to supervise the others, as she will be attending you and need an assistant to see to other matters.

+ At the rehearsal and rehearsal dinner, the Maid of Honor will cover details about the wedding day: ushering duties—(see section on Ushers) who sits where, introduce the Bridesmaids to those select individuals, inform them what time to arrive, and any special duties, such as where and when for photos.

+ At the reception, a chosen Bridesmaid may make a brief speech and/or toast.

+ They each contribute to purchase a small gift for you, the Bride.

The Day of the Wedding

Prior to the Ceremony

+ The Maid of Honor will coordinate their early arrival at the site. This is usually well before the ceremony so that last minute hair and makeup can be done.

+ They will receive any last minute instructions from her and they will again familiarize themselves with the arrangement of the site so that they can direct guests as needed (to additional parking, restrooms, any special seating needs, etc.).

+ They receive their bouquets (if any).

+ They may be asked to make certain all members of the Bride and Grooms family are wearing their corsages/boutonnieres, and verify that the Groomsmen are too. Because . . .

+ They will probably pose for the pre-wedding photographs by the wedding photographer.

+ The Maid of Honor may need their additional help assisting you with your preparations for the ceremony.

+ One Bridesmaid may be asked to supervise the flower girl and ring bearer, and prepare them for the ceremony once the children's parents have been seated.

+ They make certain that last minute preparations at the wedding venue, such as verifying the decorations and flower arrangements are set, making certain the aisle runner is ready for a Groomsman to roll out, etc.

+ They may act as ushers and/or pass out wedding programs [see the chapter *Ushers*]

+ And there most important duty: Meet with and offer their support to you, the Bride!

During the Ceremony (depending on tradition)

+ They may be escorted by their Groomsman partner, or walk out singly during the processional.

+ They stand to the left and slightly behind the Maid of Honor and you at the altar.

+ They may be escorted by their Groomsman partner, or walk out singly during the recessional.

After the Ceremony

+ They may form a processional walkway with the Groomsmen and your and the Groom's parents, as you newlyweds leave the venue.

+ One chosen Bridesmaid may assist the Maid of Honor when she leaves to quickly go to the reception site to make certain that it is ready.

   While the other Bridesmaids stay behind to…

+ Help direct guests to the reception, answer any questions, etc.

+ Help clean up the pews and collect any programs, purses, etc. left at the ceremony, roll up the aisle runner, etc. and deliver any found personal items to the reception. One or more Groomsmen will also stay to assist.

At the Reception

+ The Bridesmaid who arrived with the Maid of Honor at the reception venue will often help the arriving guests sign the guest book and direct them to the gifts table and seating chart. (She may either be asked to do this on her own or assist any Groomsman likewise assigned)

+ Bridesmaids may be asked to stand in the reception line and then, after the guests are seated, be introduced with their Groomsman escort.

+ Bridesmaids are usually seated with the Groomsmen near the Bride and Grooms table.

+ One of them will represent them all and give a very brief speech and/or toast.

+ A Bridesmaid may be asked to help the Maid of Honor carry your train and bustle it prior to dancing.

+ After the formal dances of the Bride and Groom and the parent's dances, the floor is open to everyone. Traditionally, the first dance of the Bridesmaids is with the Groomsmen who escorted them.

+ Bridesmaids are often asked to mix with the guests and dance with any unescorted male guests, serving as hosts.

+ They help encourage the unmarried women among the guests to join in the bridal bouquet toss.

+ A Bridesmaid may be asked to help you to the restroom if needed.

+ As the reception draws to a close, they usually meet briefly with you and you offer your personal thanks and present each of them with a small gift.

+ They may help the Groomsmen decorate your newlyweds "getaway car."

After the Reception

+ They may help carry the wedding gifts to the (usually) Mother of the Bride's car.

+ They help check the venue to be certain no one left anything behind.

+ If the reception was held at a private residence, they and the Groomsmen may be asked to help clean up.

+ Each Bridesmaid is individually responsible for returning any rented formalwear to the Maid of Honor or directly to the rental store.

THE BEST MAN

Also known as the Chief Groomsman, Best Person (if a female is chosen for the role) or by the gender-neutral term, Honor Attendant.

Whether he is or isn't the Grooms best friend, he is for now! He is the Groom's personal attendant, advisor, and valet. He supervises his fellow Groomsmen, making sure that they are aware of their duties and follows up to be certain those duties are performed. As the Groom's main confidant, he is also the Groomsmen's "go to" for any questions. He would contact the Groom on their behalf, as needed.

Though often the Grooms brother or best friend, whoever is chosen must be at least 18 years old, as he will be a witness to the wedding and will sign the marriage certificate.

He is the Chief Groomsman, as the Maid/Matron of Honor is the Chief Bridesmaid. As such, he is the leader among them. His position is equal to the Maid of Honor and he, therefore, shares a place of honor as the third most important members of the Wedding Party after the Bride and Groom.

His expenses

He is expected to pay for his own attire, any alterations, and accessories. If he is from out of town, he must pay his own travel expenses and accommodations, although the Groom usually arranges accommodations, often at a relatives or friends home.

He is expected to present only one small bridal shower and one personal wedding gift, his duties as Best Man being his major present for The Couple.

General Duties

Note: if the Best Man is from out of town, several of the following duties may change.

He is the primary liaison between the Groom and the Groomsmen. He is responsible for making sure that his fellow groomsmen know and understand their duties. As Chief Groomsman, he:

is responsible for the supervision of the Groomsmen and/or Ushers;
gathers the Groomsmen for the formal photos;
organizes the return of any Groomsman's rented attire.

He may also be asked to host or co-host the reception. If you choose to have him perform this additional duty, you must inform him of this and work with him as the order of events and speeches for the reception.

Prior to the Wedding

+ He works with the Groom (and, perhaps, the Bride) to outline any and all activities required of the Groomsmen in preparing for the wedding events.

+ Along with the Groom, he hosts a Groomsmen's "get together" luncheon as a "meet and greet" to introduce the groomsmen and others, discuss the wedding, and their role in making it a success.

+ He must create a list of all Groomsmen's names and phone numbers for use as needed prior to the actual ceremony. He is responsible for informing all Groomsmen not only *what* is required of them, but also *when* it is required. He may be asked by the Groom to convey additional information to them as the wedding plans progress.

+ He will also need the phone number of the Maid of Honor to coordinate information and to make certain that the wedding timeline is followed.

+ He may be asked to help plan the wedding and reception, working with the Bride, Groom, and others.

+ He may be asked by the Groom to accompany him, the Bride and others as they visit venues for both the wedding and the reception, florists, bakers, caterer's, etc. As Best Man, he is expected to give his honest opinion of places, colors, styles, tastes, etc., ***if asked for it***.

+ He coordinates any necessary activities (DIY projects, pre-wedding luncheons, etc.) involving both Groomsmen and Bridesmaids with the Maid of Honor.

+ He attends pre-wedding activities, such as the rehearsal, rehearsal dinner*, the bachelor party, etc. and sees to it that all Groomsmen attend as well, providing them with the date and times for these events and coordinating transportation, if necessary.

+ He works with his fellow Groomsmen to plan, coordinate, and pay for the Groom's bachelor party ("stag-do" or 'bucks night")—dependent on the Groom's preferences. He usually hosts this event.

+ Along with the Father of the Groom and his fellow Groomsmen, he may be asked to pick-up out of town guests; and may be asked to help arrange accommodations for any Groomsmen from out-of-town.

+ He may help the Groom shop for, choose and purchase or rent his wedding attire (although the Bride often coordinates this.) He may also be asked to both pick up and return the Groom's rented attire.

+ He pays for his own formal attire, which traditionally is the same style as the Grooms. However, often it is the Groom's decision as to how he and the Groomsmen will dress. Perhaps the Groom is in a tuxedo and the Groomsmen wear dark suits.

+ Once the preferred style is chosen for the Groomsmen, he informs them of this, the rental store phone and address, instructions for payment, etc. He organizes and coordinates the matching rentals and fittings for the Groomsmen, and reminds them to return the rental attire to him after the wedding.

+ He must attend pre-wedding events, especially both the rehearsal and rehearsal dinner, for which the Father of the Groom (the traditional host) may ask him to coordinate the speeches/toasts.

+ He reminds the Groom about the honeymoon and works with him to verify all necessary paperwork is organized, helps confirm all travel, car rental, hotel, and other reservations, he may help the Groom pack, etc.

+ As the Groom's valet, he should create and keep a "'Day of' Emergency Kit," bringing it with him on the wedding day. [See the Appendices]

+ He works with his fellow Groomsmen to select and purchase a gift for the Groom.

The Day of the Wedding

Prior to the ceremony

- He makes arrangements to get both himself and the Groom to the ceremony *at least* one hour before or earlier if formal photos are to be taken.

- He acts as Groom's valet, helping him dress and prep for the ceremony; he has the "'Day of' Emergency Kit," if needed.

- He also coordinates the on-time arrival of all Groomsmen and organizes them for the pre-ceremony photos.

- He makes certain that they are dressed correctly, have their boutonnieres through button-holes or pinned to their left lapel, etc.

- He helps gather his fellow Groomsmen for any formal photos before the ceremony.

- He confirms with the Maid of Honor that the officiant has arrived and is prepared for the ceremony.

- He is responsible for the return of the groom's personal items to the Groom's house or designated recipient.

+ He verifies and holds The Couples honeymoon paperwork (traveler's checks, passports, hotel reservations, tickets, etc.) and luggage ready for the honeymoon.

+ He also makes arrangements for the transport of The Couple after the reception, by either driving them himself or hiring a limousine or other transportation.

+ He and a Groomsman may be responsible for packing the luggage into The Couples "get away" vehicle prior to the ceremony.

+ Also as a valet, he may bring a change of clothes for the Groom to change into for the reception. Usually, the Groom will change clothes either during the reception to "dress down" for the festivities but more likely, will do so before leaving the reception to start the honeymoon.

+ He verifies there are at least two ushers (Groomsmen or hired-help) to seat the wedding guests.

+ He carries an extra copy of any special seating arrangements and makes certain that the Ushers have their copies.

+ He may supervise the ushers and verify that they have copies of and pass out any wedding programs, information on the reception, etc.

(Or he may delegate this to a trusted Groomsman.)

During the Ceremony (depending on tradition)

+ He may escort the Maid of Honor, or walk out singly during the processional.

+ He may hold the Bride's wedding ring for the Groom. (If there is a ring bearer, the rings carried are usually faux rings, the Best Man holding the real ring.)

+ At the altar, he stands to the right and slightly behind the Groom.

+ He gives the Groom the ring for the exchange of rings.

+ He escorts the Maid of Honor for the recessional.

After the Ceremony

+ He acts as a witness to the signing of the marriage certificate by The Couple, and traditionally, he and the Chief Bridesmaid sign the marriage certificate as witnesses.

+ On behalf of The Couple, he gives the wedding officiant a sealed envelope with the fee at the rehearsal or after the ceremony, as decided between the Groom (who actually pays the fee) and the officiant.

+ He may be asked to pay and thank any ushers hired as wedding staff on behalf of the Groom (who actually pays the fee).

+ He helps gather his fellow Groomsmen for any formal photos.

+ If there is no limousine and driver hired, he drives the newlyweds to the reception.

At the Reception

+ If there is a reception line at the reception, he stands next to the Bride. If not…

+ He may be announced and enter with the Maid of Honor at the reception.

+ If there is a head table, he is seated to the Bride's right.

+ Although the Father of the Bride is the traditional reception host, he may be asked to act as host for the reception or share those duties with the Father of the Bride and/or a hired

Master of Ceremonies (sometimes an additional duty of the DJ, if one was hired).

Note: if you choose to have him host or co-host the reception, you must inform him of this and work with him as the order of events and speeches for the reception.

+ Regardless, he traditionally makes a speech and/or toast to the Bride and Groom. This speech is often viewed with anticipation as the Best Man speech traditionally has elements of risqué humor and offers a break from the often "weepy" speeches that follow.*

+ If you have asked him to, he may read emails/telegrams/letters of congratulations that you have given him prior to the ceremony.

+ If there is a formal dance—After The Couple's first dance and the Bride's dance with her father and father-in-law, he will dance with the Bride; the Groom will dance with his mother and mother-in-law and then he will dance with the Maid of Honor. After this, the Best Man may be asked to encourage dancing, if there is no other wedding coordinator (host).

+ Regardless of anything else, he mingles with the guests and may dance with unaccompanied guests and unescorted Bridesmaids.

+ He encourages all bachelors to take part in the garter-tossing if the activity is held.

+ He may be asked by the Maid of Honor to help organize the bouquet toss.

+ He may be asked to assist the Father of the Bride in distributing sealed payment envelopes to the vendors, musicians, DJ, etc.

+ He (and perhaps the Maid of Honor) may be asked to collect any gift envelopes from the attendees and hold them for The Couple until their return from their honeymoon or, along with the Father of the Bride, make a deposit in The Couple's bank account. (If the latter, he notes the name and dollar amount of each gift so The Couple can send "thank you" cards.)

+ He and his fellow Groomsmen (sometimes helped by the Maid of Honor and the Brides-maids) organize the newlywed's departure and help decorate the "getaway" car.

+ If not done by the Father of the Bride (the traditional host), he and the Maid of Honor close the evening by thanking everyone for attending and wishing them farewell.

+ He verifies that two groomsmen stand on either side of the exit door and say "Good Night" (or as appropriate) to guests as they leave the reception. The Groomsmen may be assisted by two Bridesmaids.

After the Reception (or before the departure of the Bride and Groom)

+ He double-checks with the Groom to be sure that he has the tickets, passports, visas, monies/traveler's checks, etc. necessary for the honeymoon.

+ He may help load the "get away" car with The Couple's luggage, if not previously done.

+ He, the other Groomsmen, and/or the Maid of Honor may help transport the wedding gifts to the Bride's parent's house.

+ If the Groomsmen attire is rented, he contacts all Groomsmen to return them to him and he is responsible for returning them to the rental store.

+ He may also be asked to return the Grooms rented attire. If the attire was purchased, he may be asked to have it dry cleaned and return it to the Groom upon his return from the honeymoon.

+ He usually receives a personal "thank you" gift from the Groom.

+ He is usually asked to join the Father of the Bride's morning-after party if one is given.

+ Once you and your husband have returned from your honeymoon, you may ask him to help to open and to log wedding gifts, or helping you two move into and setting up a new house or apartment.

YOUR Wedding Speech Made Easy: The "How-to" Guide for the Father of the Bride, the Best Man . . . and Everyone Else! (Writing and Delivering YOUR Perfect Wedding Speech)

THE GROOMSMEN'S DUTIES

Called Ushers in the U.K.; and also known by the gender-neutral term, Honor Attendants

Groomsmen are your Groom's personal attendants. They are usually chosen from amongst his closest family and friends. They may be single or married. The Best Man is chosen from this group and is the direct liaison with the Groom. The other Groomsmen follow the directions of this Chief Groomsman.

Their expenses

If they have traveled from out of town, they traditionally pay for their own transportation, car rental, and lodging. They pay for the rental of their formalwear, any alterations, and accessories. They pay their share of the expenses for the bachelor party, and they pay a portion of the expense for the Groom's gift.

General Duties

Prior to the Wedding

+ They meet with the Groom and Best Man to cover in detail what is expected of them and to divide some of the duties in an informal Groomsmen get-together.

+ They exchange their names and phone numbers, especially with the Best Man, to expedite communication so that any last-minute changes in their particular duties can be relayed to them.

+ They work with the Best Man on organizing the rental and fittings for their tuxedos or other formal attire (which they pay for themselves).

+ They may act as chauffeurs picking up out of town guests from airports, train stations, etc. They may help the Best Man locate accommodations for the out of town guests.

+ Meet the Bridesmaids, in particular, their escort with whom they will "walk the aisle."

+ They may assist the Bridesmaids with projects, such as creating a wedding program, creating maps to the reception, decorating the ceremony and reception sites, etc.

+ They help the Best Man plan, organize, and pay for the bachelor party.

+ They attend that and any other parties—engagement, rehearsal, and reception.

+ Near the day of the ceremony, the Best Man will select one of them to supervise the others as he will attend the Groom and need an assistant to see to the other Groomsmen and other matters.

+ At the rehearsal and rehearsal dinner, the Best Man will cover details about the wedding day: ushering duties—(see section on Ushers) who sits where, introduce the groomsmen to those select individuals, inform them what time to arrive, and any special duties, such as where and when for photos.

+ At the reception, a chosen Groomsman may make a brief speech and/or toast.

+ They each contribute to purchase a small gift for the Groom.

The Day of the Wedding

Prior to the Ceremony

+ The Best Man will coordinate their early arrival at the site.

+ They will receive any last minute instructions from him and they will again familiarize themselves with the arrangement of the site so that they can direct guests as needed (to additional parking, restrooms, any special seating needs, etc.).

+ They receive and pin on their boutonniere.

+ Meet with and offer their support to the groom.

+ They will probably pose for the formal photographs by the wedding photographer.

+ The Best Man may need their help assisting the Groom with his preparations for the ceremony.

+ They may be asked to help the Bridesmaids with last-minute preparations at the venue, such as verifying the decorations and flower arrangements are set, make certain the aisle runner is rolled out (if using one) just before the processional, etc.

+ Act as ushers and/or pass out wedding programs (for these duties, see the chapter *Ushers*).

During the Ceremony (depending on tradition)

+ Either walk out with the Groom or escort their Bridesmaid partner during the processional.

+ Stand to the right and slightly behind the Best Man and Groom at the altar.

+ Escort their Bridesmaid partner during the recessional.

After the Ceremony

+ They may form a processional walkway with the Bridesmaids and parents of The Couple, as the newlyweds leave the venue.

+ One Groomsman will then leave quickly to go to the reception site to make certain that it is ready while the other(s) stay behind to…

+ They often help direct guests to the reception, answer any questions, etc.

+ Help the Bridesmaids (and/or ushers) clean up the pews and collect any programs, purses, etc. left at the ceremony, roll up the aisle runner, etc. Deliver any found personal items to the reception.

At the Reception

+ The Groomsman who arrived first at the reception venue will often help the arriving guests sign the reception book, direct them to the gifts table and seating chart, and perhaps assist in helping place the larger gifts. (A Bridesmaid may assist him.)

+ Groomsmen may be asked to stand in the reception line and then, after the guests are seated, be introduced with their Bridesmaid escort.

+ Groomsmen are usually seated near the Bride and Grooms table.

+ They may be seated together with the Bridesmaids at the table.

+ One of them will represent them all and give a very brief speech and/or toast.

+ After the formal dances of the Bride and Groom and the parent's dances, the floor is open to everyone. Traditionally, the first dance of the Groomsman is with the Bridesmaid he escorted.

+ Groomsmen are often asked to mix with the guests and dance with any unescorted guests.

+ They help encourage the bachelors among the guests to join in the garter toss if one is being performed.

+ As the reception draws to a close, they usually meet briefly with the Groom who offers his personal thanks and presents each of them with a small gift.

+ They may help the Bridesmaids decorate the newlyweds "getaway car,"

+ And help stow their luggage in the car.

After the Reception

+ One or more Groomsmen will stand near the exit doors (perhaps with the Fathers of the Bride and Groom), thank the guests for attending, and remind them to take their personal belongings.

+ They may help carry the wedding gifts to the (usually) Mother of the Bride's car.

+ Help check the venue to be certain was left behind.

+ If the reception was held at a private residence, they and the Bridesmaids may be asked to help clean up.

+ They are individually responsible for returning their rented formalwear to the Best Man.

+ You may ask one or more of them to help you and your husband move into your new house or apartment, if necessary.

THE PARENTS OF THE COUPLE

As I mentioned before, The Couple's parents have *roles* to play in both the wedding and the reception, with duties and responsibilities at each event. If a parent cannot perform these roles or fulfill these duties due to age, infirmity, distance, divorce, or decease, then you may need to choose someone(s) else must perform them. This person (or persons) may act as a proxy for the missing parent or depending on the circumstance, an actual replacement for them. If that person is a proxy, and the parent is able, the parent may then "walk the wedding" and whoever performed the duties is a special honored guest (seated with the family at the wedding, invited to the rehearsal dinner, the reception, and all other activities, etc.) If that person is replacing the parent, he or she has assumed most or all the duties of the parent and should be accorded full honors.

In the case of a divorce, if you or your Groom has remained close to your biological parent, it's completely okay to have Father*s* of the Bride, Mother*s* of the Groom, etc. and have both the biological and stepparents share some of the duties.

Your parents are your closest confidants and should have your best interests at heart, even more so than your Maid of Honor and Best Man. They should be the first people you rely on to give you advice. However, parents are sometimes reluctant to contradict their children if it seems that the Bride or Groom truly "has their heart set" on something. You need to reassure your parents that they may *always* speak openly and honestly with you about any matters concerning the wedding. They need to be able to feel that you are willing to listen to what they have to say.

Now, all of this presupposes that you and your partner have a good relationship with your parents. If you do not, whoever you have chosen as the replacement for your parent in that role in your wedding may or may not be your confidant. You may find yourself relying more on your Maid of Honor or Best Man for personal advice. If so, this is another reason to choose them carefully.

Finally, as with all of the following chapters on the members of the Wedding Party, what I have listed is not a complete list of all that they should or must do. These are mostly the primary, traditional duties and you may add or eliminate them to create a wedding that is perfect for you.

As before, I have listed the Couple's parent's joint duties first, followed by their each parents individual duties.

THE PARENTS OF THE BRIDE JOINT DUTIES

They announce their daughter's engagement, usually through a local newspaper and/or through their social media.

After that, the Parents of the Groom usually contact them and the Bride's Parents will traditionally host an informal get-together with the Groom's parents (a brunch, backyard BBQ, etc.) as both a casual meet-and-greet to introduce themselves and the Bride's family, and to unofficially discuss the wedding.

The Parents of the Groom usually reciprocate to introduce the Bride and her parents to their family.

Although the Parents of the Bride traditionally pay for both the wedding and reception, today it is more financially realistic to expect they will share the expenses either with your fiancés family, with you and him, or between all of you. Your parents need to discuss the wedding expenses with you, and then again, with you and the Groom, helping you both to establish a practical budget.

Depending on your parents' financial circumstances, they may need to curtail some traditional financial obligations, as such they may host a smaller reception or host at a less expensive venue.

I urge you not to become a "Bridezilla" and to recognize that you are fortunate to have your parents support in this and whatever they are able to do for you, I hope that you accept it graciously and with the love with which it is given.

THE PARENTS OF THE GROOM
JOINT DUTIES

Once the engagement is announced, your fiancé's parents customarily contact the Parents of the Bride to offer their formal congratulations and arrange to visit them and you, either traveling to meet you or, if traveling is an issue, conversing on the phone.

Traditionally, the Parents of the Bride will host an informal get-together with the Groom's parents (a brunch, backyard BBQ, etc.) as a casual meet-and-greet. The Parents of the Groom then likewise host a get-together for you and your parents to introduce you both to their family.

During the initial get-together, the Parents of the Groom formally offer their help with any wedding preparations.

If the Parents of the Bride are planning an engagement party for The Couple, the Parents of the Groom may ask to either co-host it, or host a second engagement party for you and their son later on.

Although the Parents of the Bride traditionally pay for the wedding and reception, today it is more financially realistic to share the expenses. The Groom's parents need to discuss the wedding expenses with their son, and then again, with him and you, helping you both set a practical budget.

Depending on the parents' financial circumstances, they may need to curtail some of their own traditional financial obligations, such as hosting the rehearsal dinner at a favorite family restaurant rather than at a country club.

Again, I urge you and your Groom to graciously accept any help, financial or otherwise, that they offer.

THE MOTHER OF THE BRIDE'S DUTIES

The Mother of the Bride is your chief confidant, support, and a shoulder to cry on. She is the "mother bear" upon which you may rely to help get through all aspects of the wedding preparation.

<u>Her expenses</u>

Traditionally, the Bride's parents foot the bill for both the wedding and the reception. However, today it is more realistic to see these expenses shared with the Groom's parents and/or The Couple.

The Mother of the Bride purchases or rents her dress and accessories.

She purchases a gift for the Bride and Groom.

General Duties

Prior to the Wedding

+ She plans and organizes the engagement party with you. And if being held jointly with your fiancé's parents, she will also work with them, most usually with the Mother of the Groom.

+ She gets the name and phone number of the Maid of Honor and Best Man for future contact.

+ She helps the Bride and Groom both research and select the wedding and reception sites, and asks friends for recommendations for caterers, bakers, florists, and other vendors.

+ She helps the Bride and the Maid of Honor both set up and maintain the Wedding Binder—the central organizational place for all the information regarding vendors, venues, costs, checklists, names, addresses, and phone numbers, etc.

+ Once it is established, she works with the Maid of Honor to make sure the wedding timeline is followed for all activities, deliveries, etc.

+ She often acts as the main contact and coordinator (or shares these duties with the Maid of Honor) for all vendors.

+ She shops with the Bride, the Maid of Honor and often the Mother of the Groom for the Bride's dress and accessories, helping her choose as appropriate.

+ She shops for her own wedding dress and accessories and informs the Mother of the Groom of her selection so that she can choose a complementary style and color.

+ She, the Maid of Honor, and the Mother of the Groom often attend the Bride's fittings.

+ She helps compile the guest list, in coordination with the Groom's Mother.

+ The Mother of the Bride is the main contact (or shares those duties with the Maid of Honor) for the bridesmaids, vis-á-vis the Bride.

+ She helps contact friends and family with information about where the Bride has her registry and may offer gift suggestions.

+ She may work with the Maid of Honor to organize the Bridal Shower.

+ The Mother of the Bride often organizes an additional get-together for the Groom's family, or for the women of both families midway to the wedding date.

+ Along with the Maid of Honor she:
Helps record the responses to the invitations; and
Helps record the receipt of gifts and who sent them in the "Gift's Log";

+ She may be responsible for bringing the guest book, unity candle (if using), and other properties needed for the ceremony and reception.

+ She attends all pre-wedding events, such as the engagement party, the rehearsal, the rehearsal dinner, etc.

+ She also works with the Mother of the Groom to research and, if possible, include any ethnic or cultural elements, and/or family traditions in the wedding ceremony and the reception.

The Day of the Wedding

Prior to the ceremony

+ Along with the Maid of Honor, she contacts the Best Man, Groomsmen, and Bridesmaids to be certain they will be ready and will arrive at their scheduled time prior to the ceremony.

+ Traditionally, she and the Father of the Bride travel with the Bride to the ceremony site.

+ She serves as the traditional hostess at the wedding, greeting guests and thanking them for attending.

+ Along with the Maid of Honor and brides-maids, may help assist the Bride with hair, make-up, etc.

+ She may assist the Maid of Honor and Brides-maids with their own dresses, hair and make-up.

+ She will organize everyone for any formal pho-tographs, both pre- and post-wedding.

+ She will often briefly meet with the Groom and the Parents of the Groom to wish them well.

+ Just before they walk to the ceremony, the Bridesmaids and Maid of Honor traditionally leave the Bride alone so that she and you can share a final, often tearful, "mommy/daughter moment" before the ceremony. She then tradi-tionally fits and adjusts the bridal veil. And will do it once again just before she enters in the processional.

During the Ceremony (depending on tradition)

+ She walks down the aisle escorted by the Father of the Bride, regardless of their present marital status. OR If both parents are divorced and remarried, she is escorted by her new husband, or a Groomsman, and is seated with the Bride's family.

After the Ceremony

+ She organizes everyone for formal photographs.

+ Often travels early to the reception site to coordinate with the Maid of Honor that everything is set. She may bring the guest book, if not already taken by the Maid of Honor.

At the Reception

+ She serves as the traditional hostess at the reception, greeting guests and thanking them for attending.

+ If there is a receiving line, the Mother of the Bride stands at its head, the Father of the Bride to her left.

+ She sits at the designated Parents' table if there is one.

+ If there is a formal dance—She dances with the Groom, and, traditionally, the Father of the Groom, and then her own husband.

+ She and the Father of the Bride socialize with the guests, especially with the Parents of the Groom.

After the Reception

+ She receives and holds all gifts from the reception until The Couple returns from the honeymoon. At which time, she and the Maid of Honor may help The Couple list who gave them what, and assists with "thank you" notes for these gifts and those listed on the "Gift's Log."

+ She and the Father of the Bride may host a morning-after party for some of the guests, especially those from out of town. This is a very casual affair, usually a small backyard brunch or picnic.

THE FATHER OF THE BRIDE'S DUTIES

Traditionally, the Father of the Bride has many duties and plays a relatively major role in the wedding preparations. As a father, he is there for you to offer suggestions and advice on both the wedding and married life. Ask of him what you will, and involve him as needed as the wedding preparations progress. After all, and at the very least, most Father's of the Bride have a financial interest in the wedding

Usually, the Bride's biological parent fills the role of Father of the Bride. However, in the case of divorce or decease, it may be a stepfather or any (usually older) male relative. Whoever it is, he traditionally "gives away" the Bride into the care of the bridegroom.

His expenses

While tradition dictates that he pay for the wedding ceremony and reception, today it is more likely that the expenses are shared with the Groom's parents and/or The Couple (many of whom foot the bill themselves).

The Father of the Bride pays for his formal wear purchase or rental, as well as a gift for The Couple.

General Duties

Prior to the Wedding

+ He may help the Father of the Groom, the Best Man and other Groomsmen with planning wedding transportation, and locating and reserving lodgings for out-of-town guests (perhaps at a hotel or with family and friends)

+ He might assist in creating maps and directions to the wedding and reception venues for use as inclusions with the wedding invitations and pass outs at the wedding site

+ Attends pre-wedding events, such as the engagement party, the rehearsal, the rehearsal dinner, etc.

+ At the engagement party and rehearsal dinner, he makes a brief toast welcoming the Groom into the family and . . .

+ He makes a formal speech and toast at the reception, which he traditionally hosts—or co-hosts with the Best Man.*

+ He may be asked to help prepare the guest list.

+ He should coordinate his attire with the Groom (match or contrast, as decided; the attire may or may not be the same as chosen for the Groomsmen) and rents or purchases as necessary.

+ He may be asked to attend the bachelor party, though this is rare.

The Day of the Wedding

Prior to the ceremony

+ Traditionally, he and the Mother of the Bride travel with the Bride to the ceremony site.

+ He will pose for any formal photographs.

+ He will often briefly meet with the Groom and the Parents of the Groom to wish them well.

+ Just before they walk to the ceremony, the Bridesmaids and Maid of Honor traditionally leave the Bride alone so that he and the Bride can share a final, often tearful, "daddy/daughter moment" before the ceremony.

During the Ceremony (depending on tradition)

+ He escorts the Bride down the aisle and "gives her away" to the Groom, then takes his designated seat, usually beside the Mother of the Bride.

After the Ceremony

+ Stays for formal photographs and those of guests.

At the Reception

Note: Although the Father of the Bride is the traditional host of the reception, nowadays it is more likely that he will co-host, sharing many of the duties with the Maid of Honor and/or Best Man; a professional MC (often the DJ), and/or the wedding coordinator (if there is one).

+ If there is a receiving line, he stands to the left of the Mother of the Bride

+ He sits at the designated Parents' table if there is one.

+ He will often open the reception by making a short welcome speech.*

+ Later, he will make a longer speech saluting the Bride and Groom, thanking everyone, and then toasting the Bride and Groom*

+ If there is a formal dance—He dances with his daughter, the Bride, and traditionally, later with the Mother of the Groom, and, of course, his own wife.

+ He socializes with his new in-laws, the Groom's family

+ As the traditional host of the reception, he supervises all reception activities, the food, the drinks, and bar, etc. Most often though, these duties are performed by the Maid of Honor and Best Man.

+ He and the Mother of the Bride socialize, especially with the parents of the Groom

After the Reception

+ He may host a morning-after party for some of the guests, especially those from out of town, the parents of the Groom, the Maid of Honor and Best Man. This is a very casual affair, usually a small backyard brunch or picnic.

*YOUR Wedding Speech Made Easy: The "How-to" Guide for the Father of the Bride, the Best Man . . . and Everyone Else! (Writing and Delivering YOUR Perfect Wedding Speech)

THE MOTHER OF THE GROOM'S DUTIES

Though the Mother of the Groom has traditionally had few real duties, today things are often quite different. Nowadays the Mother of the Groom actively participates in the wedding preparations and, especially if the Groom's family is sharing the wedding expenses, will often share duties with the Mother of the Bride.

Her expenses

Traditionally, the Groom's parents pay for the rehearsal dinner and the bar tab at the reception. However, today it is more realistic to see these expenses shared with the Bride's parents and/or The Couple.

The Mother of the Groom purchases or rents her dress and accessories and purchases a gift for the Bride and Groom.

<u>General Duties</u>

Prior to the Wedding

+ She may host a dinner to introduce the Bride to the Groom's side of the family. As well as host a second one for the Parents of the Bride.

+ She will help locate ceremony and wedding reception venues and research caterers, bakers, florists, and other vendors.

+ She will offer to serve as an additional contact for the wedding vendors.

+ She shops with the Bride, the Maid of Honor, and the Mother of the Bride for the Bride's dress and accessories, helping her choose as appropriate.

+ She may shop with or contact the Mother of the Bride about her formal wear so that she chooses attire that complements the style and color chosen by the Mother of the Bride.

+ She will create a guest list for the Groom's family, working with the Bride and the Mother of the Bride to make certain the numbers of guests are acceptable.

+ She attends all pre-wedding events, such as the engagement party, the bridal shower, the rehearsal, the rehearsal dinner, etc.

+ She also works with the Mother of the Bride to research and, if possible, include any ethnic or cultural elements, and/or family traditions in the wedding ceremony and the reception.

+ She helps contact friends and family with information about where The Couple is registered and may make gift suggestions.

+ She helps organize, plan, and helps host the Rehearsal dinner with the Father of the Groom.

The Day of the Wedding

Prior to the ceremony

+ Traditionally, she and the Father of the Groom both travel with the Groom to the ceremony site.

+ She will pose for formal photographs.

+ She may be asked by the Bride and/or the Mother of the Bride to assist with the Bride's hair, makeup, and other preparations.

+ She will often briefly meet with the Bride and the Parents of the Bride to wish them well.

+ Just before they walk to the ceremony, the Groomsmen traditionally leave the Groom alone so that she and her son can share a final, often tearful, "mother/son moment" before the ceremony. She also traditionally places and adjusts the Groom's boutonniere.

During the Ceremony—depending on tradition

+ She walks down the aisle escorted by the Father of the Bride, regardless of their present marital status. OR if both parents are divorced and remarried, she is escorted by her new husband, or a Groomsman and sits with the Groom's family.

After the Ceremony

+ She poses for both the formal and informal photos.

+ She may leave for the reception a little early to assist the Mother of the Bride and the Maid of Honor with any last minute preparations.

At the Reception

+ She and the Father of the Groom socialize with the guests, especially with the Parents of the Bride.

+ If there is a receiving line, she stands to the left of the Bride's parents.

+ She sits at the designated Parents' table (if there is one).

+ If there is a formal dance, she dances with her son, the Groom, and then with the Father of the Bride, and then her husband.

After the Reception

+ She may be asked to join the Father of the Bride's morning-after party if one is given.

THE FATHER OF THE GROOM'S DUTIES

Traditionally, the Father of the Groom has few duties and plays only a relatively minor role in the wedding preparations. In other words, he gets away pretty darn lucky!

As a father, he is there for his son to offer suggestions and advice on the wedding and married life. Of course, if he is also helping finance the wedding, he is certainly more involved than I've indicated. Some Fathers of the Groom are often reluctant to offer help, but after all, he will soon be your father-in-law, so involve him, make him feel both wanted and a valuable part of the wedding prep!

His expenses

Traditionally, he pays for the rehearsal dinner and the beverage/bar tab for the reception. Again, this may be an expense shared with your parents and/or you and your Groom.

He pays for his formal wear purchase or rental, as well as a gift for The Couple.

General Duties

Prior to the Wedding

+ Coordinates attire with the Groom (match or contrast, as decided; may or may not be the same as chosen for the Groomsmen) and rents or purchases as necessary.

+ He may be asked to help the Groom and Bride scout venues and suppliers.

+ Along with the Mother of the Groom, he suggests guests to attend the wedding and reception.

+ He may help the Father of the Groom, the Best Man and other Groomsmen with planning wedding transportation, and locating and reserving lodgings for out-of-town guests (perhaps at a hotel or with family and friends).

+ He attends pre-wedding events, such as the engagement party, the rehearsal, the rehearsal dinner, etc.

<u>The Rehearsal Dinner</u>

+ Organizes, plans, and pays for the rehearsal dinner as a "thank you" for the members of the Wedding Party.

+ As the traditional host, he makes a speech of welcome to the guests and he makes the first toast to the Groom (as a proud father), to the Bride (to welcome her to the family), then to The Couple (wishing them both a long and happy marriage).*

+ He may help plan the Bachelor Party along with the Best Man, though this is usually rare. Rarer still, he attends the bachelor party (at least appropriate parts of it).

The Day of the Wedding

Prior to the ceremony

+ Traditionally, he and the Mother of the Groom travel with the Groom to the ceremony site.

+ He meets with the Best Man to verify the arrival and appropriate attire of the Groomsmen and/or ushers.

+ He will pose for any formal photographs.

+ He will often briefly meet with the Parents of the Bride to wish them well. Like the Groom, he traditionally is not supposed to see the Bride before the ceremony.

+ Just before they walk to the ceremony, the Groomsmen and Best Man traditionally leave the Groom alone so he and his dad can share a final, often tearful, "father/son moment" before the ceremony.

During the Ceremony (depending on tradition)

+ Walks the Mother of the Groom down the aisle to their seats, regardless of their present marital status OR if both parents are divorced and remarried, he escorts his new wife and the Mother of the Groom walks escorted by new husband. If she has not remarried, she is usually escorted by a Groomsman or usher.

After the Ceremony

+ He stays for formal and informal photographs.

+ He then escorts his wife to the reception.

At the Reception

+ If there is a receiving line, he stands to the left of the Mother of the Groom.

+ He sits at the designated Parents' table if there is one.

+ If there is a formal dance—He dances with the Bride, the Mother of the Bride, and, of course, his own wife.

+ He often makes a speech and/or toast at the reception. *

+ He and the Mother of the Groom socialize with the guests, especially with the Parents of the Bride.

+ As he traditionally pays for the beverages, he supervises the drinks and bar.

After the Reception

+ Along with the Father of the Bride, he is one of the last to leave the reception and he verifies all bills are settled (traditionally, he pays for the beverages/bar).

+ He may be asked to join the Father of the Bride's morning-after party if one is given.

*YOUR Wedding Speech Made Easy: The "How-to" Guide for the Father of the Bride, the Best Man . . . and Everyone Else! (Writing and Delivering YOUR Perfect Wedding Speech)

JUNIOR ATTENDANTS

Also known as Junior Bridesmaids and Junior Groomsmen, or by the gender-neutral term, Junior Honor Attendants

Junior attendants are young children, usually, ages 5 to 15. Many people consider a child aged 16 and up to be old enough to be an actual Bridesmaid or Groomsman.

As these youngsters are children, their parents *must* be asked to accept the invitation for their child to participate in your wedding. Always make certain you have their permission *before* you approach the child to ask them to be a Junior Bridesmaid or Junior Groomsman.

And remember, the child must be mature enough to fulfill the duties required of them. It's up to you to judge this, along with input from the child's parents.

Make certain that your Maid of Honor and Best Man, as appropriate, advise the parents of all events, times, places, etc.—especially the information for the day of the wedding ceremony. The parents must have the child dressed and ready to go on time and at the appropriate place.

Their expenses

You need to make certain that the parents understand the financial obligations of accepting the invitation. This usually includes the cost of any formalwear, footwear, and accessories for the wedding; and possibly any travel and lodging expenses.

Note:

An older Junior Bridesmaid and/or Junior Groomsman may need to become an informal babysitter for the younger ones prior to and just after the ceremony. If an adult (often the mother or father of a Junior) is already supervising the smaller children, the selected Junior(s) will assist.

Often the oldest Junior Bridesmaid will be asked to supervise the other Junior Bridesmaids and report directly to the Maid of Honor, and the oldest Junior Groomsman asked to do the same for his fellows, reporting directly to the Best Man. Their position should be made known to the parents of these other Juniors, so the parents are aware of the supervisor. These supervisory duties would include headcounts to make certain that their fellows are present at the correct time and place, are dressed properly, have their flower, bouquet, corsage or boutonniere—as appropriate, line up correctly for the processional, and generally assist the Maid of Honor or Best Man in keeping all the Juniors organized and ready to participate.

Remember, Bride and Groom: Both Junior Bridesmaids and Junior Groomsmen receive small gifts from you thanking them for their participation! Make it thoughtful and age appropriate. Check with the parents for some ideas. Generally, appropriate gifts may include gift cards to a favorite eatery or store; gift cards to a movie theater; books or music suitable for that particular child's tastes, etc.

.   .   .

Junior Bridesmaids are younger members of the Wedding Party, usually nine to fourteen years old. At those ages, they have the maturity to assist the Maid of Honor and Bridesmaids with their duties—although, for the younger ones, the position is mostly honorary.

They may assist any Honorary Bridesmaids in many duties. Often they are asked to assist as ushers or pass out wedding programs at the ceremony.

If you want them to wear formal wear, it is an expense borne by their parents—as would be any hair and makeup. Some parents might be honored you asked, but can't afford the expense. Thus, it might be preferable to have them dress in a dress that is age appropriate and similar in color to that of the Bridesmaids, and Mom can always help with hair and makeup. Like the Honorary Bridesmaids, they too wear a corsage.

Because of their age, some couple's think it better to hold a small, separate "thank you" party for both them and their parents (along with the Junior Groomsmen and their parents) rather than have them attend the rehearsal dinner and the adult-oriented bachelorette/bachelor party. Others prefer to have them attend events like the bridal shower (be careful, as this event can become a little risqué!) and the rehearsal dinner. An older Junior Bridesmaid (along with an older Junior Groomsman) can always "babysit" the younger juniors, such as the flower girl and ring bearer at the rehearsal dinner and other events.

Both Honorary and Junior Bridesmaids can assist with craftwork and DIY projects—like favor making, preparing wedding invitations, cleaning up after the events they attend, and other tasks.

If you so choose, the Junior Bridesmaids may also walk the aisle with a Junior Groomsman and stand at the altar, aside from and slightly behind the Bridesmaids and Groomsmen.

Note: If the Junior Bridesmaid is your or your Grooms own child, you may wish to have her wear a bridesmaid's dress (in her size, of course), stand between you and the Maid of Honor at the altar, and include her in any personal vows you and your Groom may exchange. Likewise, you may do this for any younger child of your partner.

[For the ushering duties of Junior Attendants, see the chapter on *Ushers*.]

General Duties: Junior Bridesmaid

Prior to the Wedding:

+ Junior Bridesmaids may attend any pre-wedding events, such as the bridesmaids' luncheon, the rehearsal and rehearsal dinner, and—if age appropriate— the bridal shower, etc.

The Day of the Wedding:

Prior to the ceremony

+ Jr. Bridesmaids often wear the same style dress as the Bridesmaids. Or they may wear a different style, but in the same hue and color as the Bridesmaids.

+ They meet with a designated Bridesmaid to learn of any last minute changes (if any) to the ceremony and to receive final instructions

+ Jr. Bridesmaids carry often carry a flower or small bouquet, or wear a corsage in the Bride's choice of flower. This helps distinguish them from other children who may be guests at the wedding.

During the ceremony (depending on tradition)

+ They may walk the aisle with the Bridesmaids during the processional or be escorted by a Junior Groomsman.

+ They stand slightly behind and to the side of the Bridesmaids during the ceremony.

+ They exit the ceremony with the Bridesmaids during the recessional, perhaps escorted by a Junior Groomsman.

After the Ceremony

+ They may be asked to hand out send-off properties (such as confetti, bubbles, etc.) to the guests for use when The Couple exits the ceremony or for use later at the reception.

At the Reception:

+ At the reception, they may be asked to stand in the receiving line or enter with a Junior Groomsman, and they will be encouraged to dance at the appropriate time.

After the Reception:

+   If their parents allow, they may stay and help the Bridesmaids and Groomsmen in cleaning the venue.

. . .

Junior Groomsmen are younger members of the Wedding Party, usually nine to fifteen years old. At those ages, they are mature enough to assist the Best Man and Groomsmen with their duties. They may assist any Honorary Groomsmen in their duties. Often the primary duty of the Junior Groomsmen is that of Ushers. They may be asked to wear formal wear, an expense borne by their parents, though it might be preferable to have them dress in dark suits and be distinguished from guests by their boutonnieres. Because of their age, it is often better to hold a small, separate "thank you" party for both them and the Junior Bridesmaids, rather than have them attend the rehearsal dinner and the adult-oriented bachelor/bachelorette party. As you choose, they may also walk the aisle with a Junior Bridesmaid and stand at the altar, aside from and slightly behind the Groomsmen.

An older Junior Groomsman (along with an older Junior Bridesmaid) might be asked to "babysit" the younger Junior Groomsmen, Junior Bridesmaids, flower girl and ring bearer at the rehearsal dinner.

Both Honorary and Junior Groomsmen can assist the Groom and Best Man with a variety of tasks.

[For the ushering duties of Junior Groomsmen, see the chapter on *Ushers*.]

General Duties: Junior Groomsmen

Prior to the Wedding:

+ Junior Groomsmen may attend any pre-wedding events, such as the Groomsmen get-together, the rehearsal and rehearsal dinner, etc. However, they do not attend the bachelor party, as it is unlikely to be age appropriate.

The Day of the Wedding:

+ Jr. Groomsmen usually wear a tuxedo or a dark suit.

+ Jr. Groomsmen wear the same boutonnieres as the other Groomsmen.

+ They may perform usher duties if ages 8 and older.

+ Depending on the ceremony, they may walk the aisle with the other Groomsmen during the processional, perhaps escorting a Junior Bridesmaid.

+ They stand slightly behind and to the side of the Groomsmen during the ceremony.

+ They exit the ceremony with the Groomsmen during the recessional, perhaps escorting a Junior Bridesmaid.

After the Ceremony

+ They may be asked to hand out send-off properties (such as confetti, bubbles, etc.) to the guests for use when The Couple exits either the ceremony or the reception.

At the Reception:

+ At the reception, they may be asked to stand in the receiving line or enter with a Junior Bridesmaid, and they will be encouraged to dance with their escort at the appropriate time.

After the Reception:

+ If their parents allow, they may stay and help assist the Bridesmaids and Groomsmen in cleaning the venue.

A Special Note if the Junior Bridesmaid or Junior Groomsman is YOUR Child

If you are involving your own son or daughter in the ceremony, you certainly want to make them as involved as possible and comfortable in the role they will play. You might consider the following:

+ A very young son might be the Ring Bearer or a very young daughter, the Flower Girl. A slightly older son and/or daughter might be your trainbearer.

+ A slightly older child (boy *or* girl) can escort you down the aisle along with the Father of the Bride or, depending on circumstances, in place of him. An older son may do the same. He then stands next to the Best Man at the altar.

+ If this child is your older son, you may wish to have him wear a tuxedo (in his size, of course), stand beside your Groom and his Best Man at the altar, and include him in any personal vows that you and your Groom may exchange. Likewise, you may do this for the son of your partner.

+ An older daughter should walk in procession just before the Maid of Honor and should stand next to her at the altar. [Of course, if she is old enough, you may have chosen her *as* your Maid of Honor!]

+ If it is part of your ceremony, your child might also be a Reader of either a religious text or an appropriate poem.

If you have no children but your fiancé does, the above may be appropriate, depending on personal circumstance. However, it is certainly appropriate for a son to walk with his father down the aisle, and/or to stand beside the Best Man at the altar. His daughter may well act as a Bridesmaid and should walk just before the Maid of Honor in the procession.

If you *both* have children participating in the ceremony, it's really up to you to find a position for them. If you both have daughters, then usually the Bride's daughter walks just before the Maid of Honor, and the Groom's daughter just before her. If you both have sons, then the Grooms' son stands next to the Best Man and the Bride's son, next to him. Of course, either a son or daughter may be a Reader.

If you wish to include a child (children) in the wedding ceremony exchange of vows, the following is a suggestion from my book, *The Tao of the Vow: The Path to YOUR Perfect Vows – How to Write and Deliver YOUR Wedding Vows*

". . . marriages sometimes
mean that there are children, and it
is always preferable, with both

their consent and understanding, to include them in the ceremony. Such participation is particularly important for younger children. The children's involvement will certainly impress upon them their importance to both you and your new partner.

"One way to do this is to include them in *your* vows, such as a simple statement of love and respect for them and to welcome them into the family.

"You might also consider having them actually participate in the vows ceremony.

"With the approval of the officiant, (this is especially necessary for a religious ceremony) you and your partner may wish to recite your vows first and then have the children come forward and respond to the vow questions posed by the officiant, perhaps something like:

Officiant: "Will you accept, love, respect, and abide by your parents?"
Children: "I/We will."

Officiant: "Will you accept, respect, and cherish your new family relationship?"
Children: "I/We will."

And, if applicable:

Officiant: "Will you accept your new siblings, and always show each other love, respect, and understanding?"
Children: "We will."

"Volunteer" Attendants

Volunteer Attendants are referred to as attendants, but in reality, they are *assistants* to you and the members of the Wedding Party. The term Volunteer Attendant is mostly ceremonial. It's a polite way to acknowledge their help and include them in the wedding without actually including them in the wedding.

On average, most U.S. Couple's have only six attendants: the Maid of Honor, the Best Man, two Bridesmaids and two Groomsmen. So how do they get all the work done that needs to be done? They get "volunteers" to help.

I know that Bridesmaids and Groomsmen accepted your invitation and so are true volunteers, so who are *these* volunteers? Well, they may be your and your Groom's siblings, family, or friends and acquaintances who help, sometimes a little reluctantly—that's why the quotation marks around the word volunteers.

They may, perhaps, supplement the duties of the members of the Wedding Party, assist them as additional help is needed or perform functions that members of the Wedding Party cannot. Perhaps they act as a local driver for an out-of-town guest, or the person who runs to the tuxedo shop to pick up the Groom's tux if he or the Best Man can't. They might be part of the crew that helps both set up and clean up the "day after the wedding get-together" for select family members and out-of-town guests.

They might be someone with a special skill needed for the wedding (how to set up a sound system, how to set up and maintain an online wedding site, etc.). Or perhaps it's an Aunt who makes baked goods for the engagement party and the other get-togethers that you'll have.

These "volunteers" may assist all the time, or be "on call" as you need them and their special skill. Whoever they are and whatever they do, they are essential to your having the wedding you want.

Because they are integral to your wedding, they should be recognized for all of their hard work. However, since they are usually not invited to the wedding and/or the reception, many Couple's choose to have a party to thank them. This should be a simple, informal picnic at a park or on the beach or a backyard barbeque. Some beer, a little booze, burgers, and beans, music and dancing, all hosted by the Bride and Groom allows for a more personal and touching show of appreciation than a formal sit-down dinner.

To make the event even more special for these volunteers, both you and the Groom should make short speeches personally thanking everyone for their help. And beyond special, the both of you should make it <u>fun</u>!

One couple I know took digital photos during the work meetings and get-togethers, and printed several, arranging them on a large poster board. Their guests were delighted to see themselves "at work" and shared memories of all that they had accomplished. The Couple also bought medals and ribbons from a party goods store and awarded them as funny honors, "To the person who actually managed to go fifteen minutes without using their cell phone." "To my Grandma who went through one whole get-together without saying, 'When I was your age…'" and so on.

In addition, they handed out goody bags that contained Hershey's Kisses (that they announced were "kisses" from the both of them), an instant win scratch-off lottery ticket, the same wedding favors that would be given to the guests at the reception, and a personal, handwritten note of thanks, signed by the both of them.

Whatever *you* choose to do, thank them and recognize the remarkable work that these people have done in helping you create the wedding you want!

HONORARY ATTENDANTS

Honorary attendants are those chosen by the Bride and Groom for special recognition. Although they will not stand with you during the wedding ceremony, they are special people in your lives, perhaps friends, siblings, or family members (often grandparents or favorite aunts and uncles) who deserve appreciation, acknowledgment, and your gratitude.

It truly is an honor to be valued by you as someone of exceptional personal importance and to be rewarded with this title and position. Because of this, do not make all your friends and close family Honorary Attendants. Reserve this title for only a select few.

. . .

Honorary Bridesmaids

They may not be ceremonial Bridesmaids, but they *are* Bridesmaids. They are those friends and/or family members important to you, but who will not stand with you during the ceremony. No matter how many attendants you have for your wedding, you may still need the services of these trusted family and friends for ancillary duties.

Unfortunately, asking someone to be an Honorary Bridesmaid is often viewed as somewhat of an insult. Some women mistakenly believe that they were a second-tier choice, not good enough to be chosen as a "real" Bridesmaid. This misunderstanding can ruin relationships!

You can usually avoid problems if you make these persons understand that you only have a certain number of Bridesmaids' positions, but you still want to honor your special friends and assistants.

Make them understand that it should be considered a reward for those special persons who have helped you prepare for your wedding. Remind them also that they are still Bridesmaids, except that they will not be standing with you during the ceremony.

If you explain that you greatly appreciate all that they have done to make your special day even more special and that you wish them to understand how very much that means to you, most will be flattered that you asked them to participate as an Honorary Bridesmaid.

However, if you feel uncomfortable doing this, many Brides choose to reserve this title for their partner's sisters, or for their and their partner's older female family members, such as grandmothers and aunts.

There is little expense for an Honorary Bridesmaid, as they are not usually required to rent formal wear to match that of the Bridesmaids. Instead, just ask them to choose a similar style and color as that of your Bridesmaids, and are usually identified by their distinctive corsage.

However, choosing several Honorary Bridesmaids might increase *your* expenses. Honorary Bridesmaids attend both the ceremony and the reception, thus increasing both your number of guests and the resultant costs. Also, though they do not carry flowers, as your Bridesmaids might, the Bride usually provides them with a corsage made of the same flowers as the Bridesmaids carry, an additional floral expense. Still, if they are worthy enough to be honored, you should be willing to bear these additional expenses.

While your Honorary Bridesmaids do not receive personal gifts from you, most couples host a special get-together for them, be it a sit-down dinner or a casual backyard event. As co-hosts, both you and your partner will make a short speech thanking them for their time, effort, and assistance.

Honorary Groomsmen

They may not be ceremonial groomsmen, but they *are* Groomsmen. They are those others on the Grooms list who are still important to him, but will NOT participate in the ceremony, usually because the wedding is too small for him to have a large number of attendants. However, he still needs the services of trusted family and friends for ushers and ancillary duties. Alternatively, the Groom may have many attendants because it is a large wedding but still need extra men to perform ushering duties. These men are often younger siblings, other relatives, the Bride's brother(s), or perhaps a grandfather or favorite uncle. A position as Honorary Groomsman usually presents them with little expense, as these are often local family and friends and they are not usually required to rent formal wear. Instead, they wear a dark colored suit, their position identified by their each wearing a distinctive boutonniere.

Although their primary duty is often to act as ushers, if the Groom selected these men, they are "Honorary Groomsmen." This is an important distinction, because, at some venues, ushers may be strangers just hired as wedding staff.

· · ·

Honorary Bridesmaids and Groomsmen —

+   Do _not_ attend the rehearsal or rehearsal dinner.

+   They _are_ invited to the wedding ceremony and the reception.

+   Are most often seated with the family or in the pews immediately behind the family.

+   Are usually listed on the wedding program, if there is one.

+ Are usually acknowledged by either the Best Man or the Maid of Honor during their reception speech when they thank the Bridesmaids and Groomsmen. And again during the Bride's speech when you do the same. Usually, you and your Groom say something like, "I would also like to thank the Honorary Bridesmaids and Groomsmen for their tremendous help in making today/tonight possible." If there are only a few, you might mention them by name.

USHERS

Please note: This section contains information about escorting guests. For U.K. readers, see the chapter on *Groomsmen*.

Also, if yours is a casual or very small wedding, you may prefer to skip having ushers and include these duties as part of the Groomsmen's responsibilities or simply allow your guests to seat themselves.

You should try to have at least two Ushers for every thirty guests, but there is no real rule. Therefore, if you have several extra older Junior Groomsmen or older Junior Bridesmaids as Ushers, well, the more the merrier (usually!). It is certainly advisable to have an older Groomsman or Honorary Groomsman supervise the

Ushers, whoever they are. This is especially true if yours is a large wedding and the Ushers are hired help.

Though traditionally chosen from the Groom's side of the family, today most couple's think it's better to have Ushers from both the Bride's and Groom's family as this assures that guests from both families will see "a familiar face" when they arrive. However, Ushers may or may not be Groomsmen (honorary, junior or otherwise).

It is important to remember that an Usher is never merely "an Usher." They are the face of the wedding; often the first faces the guests see at the ceremony. They are individuals selected by you and your partner because of their friendship, maturity, and reliability. They are your welcoming committee and should be seen as a valued part of the wedding experience for both you and your guests.

Whomever you've selected to perform this service for the wedding guests, they need to be mature enough to understand the following:

+ The Head Usher should know the guest list and should know about how many guests will attend from both yours and your partner's family and friends. This will give you an indication of the seating on each side of the aisle. If there is an overflow between Bride's side or Groom's side, or if the Head Usher sees that one side of the venue is becoming too full, let him know that he has permission to begin seating the remaining guests on the other side.

+ They should arrive at least an hour before the guests. This allows for any last minute instructions.

+ They may or may not be dressed the same as the Groomsmen. Whether formalwear or dark suit, they must wear the boutonnieres you've selected to distinguish themselves.

+ They must understand the venue and be able to direct guests to water fountains, restrooms, additional parking, and answer the guest's general questions.

+ Prior to the arrival of the guests, they may be asked to help arrange seating, if chairs are used, assist the Bridesmaids and Groomsmen in any last minute tasks at the venue, etc.

+ They may also be included in the wedding photographs.

+ They must be personable and greet the guests with a smile.

+ They distribute the wedding program (if any) and/or provide information about the reception. This might be a task for a Junior Groomsman or Junior Bridesmaid, as this allows the older Ushers to act as escorts.

+ Their main role is to escort guests to their seats. As they do so, they should always smile.

To that end, they must know the venue, and who is to be seated where. It is the duty of the Head Usher to inform them of the arrangements.

Often the first few rows of each side of the aisle are reserved for members of the Bride and Grooms immediate family and closest friends. These may be designated by a small bouquet or colored bow on the sides of the row. It is up to the Best Man to have a Groomsman or older Honorary Groomsman there to supervise and let all the Ushers know who these people are. Sometimes these extra special guests can be identified by a distinctive or different color corsage or boutonniere. If so, the Ushers should be so informed.

If you have divorced parents attending the ceremony, let the Ushers know that traditionally the biological father would sit in the row behind the Mother of the Bride or Mother of the Groom. However, if they are friendly with both their ex-spouse and her/his new spouse (if any), they can be seated in the same row.

+ Ushers traditionally ask the arriving guests, "Are you a guest of the Bride or Groom?" and escort them as appropriate.

+ For most Christian services, the guests of the Bride sit on the left, and the guests of the Groom sit on the right. For a Jewish ceremony, it is the opposite. However, as some consider a marriage as the joining of two families, seating may be "open." If this is the way you've planned it, please inform the ushers NOT to ask guests, "Bride or Groom?"

+ It is important that The Couple let the Ushers know of any special needs: elderly or handi-capped guests, the possibility of seating con-flicts between divorced guests, etc.

Let the Ushers know that following is the usual way to escort guests:

When escorting a <u>female guest and her compan-ion</u>, the Usher traditionally always offers his arm to the woman. At the row the Usher steps aside, allowing her "plus one" to enter first, then allowing her to enter the row.

If a <u>female arrives alone</u>, the Usher offers his arm and escorts her.

Please *Note:* some women may not accept the offer of an arm from an Usher, if so instruct the Ushers to simply lead the way and walk the woman to her seat.

If a <u>male arrives alone</u>, it is customary to say, "Please follow me" and escort him to his seat.

If <u>a couple or family arrives</u>, the Usher should of-fer his arm to the woman in the party and es-cort them to their seats.

If there are several women in the group, it is traditional for the Usher to offer his arm to the oldest woman in the group.

If possible, families with small children and elderly guests should be seated near the aisle for their convenience and those of the others in the row.

+ As the ceremony nears its start, the Head Usher usually remains by the entrance to silently direct any late guests to the last rows. He will also open the doors for the processional and the recessional.

+ Your ceremony may be different, so inform the Ushers of the actual procedure but the following is the usual order:

Once the guests are seated, any special honored family members, such as grandparents, may be escorted to their seats.

The Parents of the Groom are usually escorted next.

After them, the Head Usher escorts the Mother of the Bride, though sometimes she is escorted by the Best Man.

After that, the Ushers' job is over except...

+ After the ceremony is complete, the Ushers traditionally dismiss the guests from the front rows first, working their way back to the doors of the venue.

After the last guest has left, you may have the Ushers help the Groomsmen and Bridesmaids with their tasks straightening and cleaning up the venue. Once that is complete, if the Ushers are members of your or your Grooms family, or are friends you've asked to help, they are almost always invited to the reception.

Note: However, if the Ushers were persons hired as wedding staff, they have been either paid in advance or are then paid and thanked by the Best Man, on behalf of the Couple, and then dismissed.

In Conclusion

Though choosing your Wedding Party is but one thing in preparing for your ceremony and reception, it is the linchpin holding everything else together. That is why it is essential that you pay attention to this important aspect of your wedding preparation to avoid problems.

And while choosing and using your Wedding Party may seem a Herculean task, now that you have read this book, I'm certain that you have a better understanding of not only how to choose your attendants, but how to use your team to help you fulfill your unique vision for your wedding. I also know that while the entire process may seem intimidating, you know that if you truly want your wedding-day dreams realized, it is something that you *must* pursue. And now you know how!

In my forty years of helping couple's, I have seen wrong choices ruin both the wedding plans and friendships. So remember, choose wisely and create your perfect Wedding Party. After all, it's *your* wedding. *You* choose your team. *You* are in charge of *your* wedding; so *you* make the tough decisions. It is better to step on a few toes than to give in to family or peer-pressure and possibly ruin your plans for your vision of the perfect wedding.

Stay strong. Be a brave Bride. You and your partner owe it to yourselves to have the greatest wedding in the world!

I conclude as I began:

You won't have the wedding you want without getting the help you need! And I'm certain that this book can help you decide whom to choose and how best to use your team.

I offer you my sincere Best Wishes; Good Luck; Great Happiness; and May Your God Go With You!

<u>NOTES</u>

APPENDICES

"Day Of" Emergency Kit

As the Bride's chief maid and the Groom's valet, the Maid of Honor and the Best Man should be prepared to help you and your fiancé with any last minute clothing or personal care emergencies. The following is a short list of things you should make certain they have with them "just in case."

For both the Bride and Groom:

Healthy Snacks:
granola or energy bars
plain bottled water (tea, coffee, or flavored powder mix-ins may stain your teeth). At least three bottles—two for you and one for them

Clothing Care:
lint roller, sewing kit, scissors, safety pins, stain removal pen

Medical Care:
antacids (both liquid and chewable tablets), aspirin (or other headache relief medicine), bandages (think blisters

from new shoes!), anti-bacterial spray, cotton balls, cotton swabs

Personal Care:
facial tissues (expect a few good cries!)
razor and shaving cream/depilatory, cologne/perfume
tweezers, nail file
hairspray or gel
facial wipes, body spray/deodorant
toothbrush, toothpaste, mouthwash, dental floss, breath mints
lip balm, skin lotion, hand sanitizer
eye care: eye drops (to remove redness), an extra set of contacts or glasses, an eyeglass repair kit, including lens wipes

Miscellaneous:
Super Glue, notebook, pencil and pen (both a black and blue ink pen for signing the marriage certificate and any other official documents), and—most importantly—additional copies of any original vows and the reception speeches that have been written

In addition, for the Bride:

Makeup Kit:
mirror compact with face powder, eyeliner, mascara, lipstick, clear nail polish, etc. for touchups; makeup remover for after the reception, makeup wipes

Personal Care:
tampons and other feminine hygiene products

Non-Western Traditions

Brides and Grooms always need help preparing for their wedding. Indeed, having people help the Bride and Groom and their families prepare for a wedding exists throughout all cultures and religions. Sometimes the preparation is material—the clothing for the ceremony, the food, preparing a place for the newlyweds to live, etcetera. Sometimes it's spiritual—undergoing spiritual preparation for the marriage, meeting with a religious leader, following religious rites and traditions, etcetera.

Here are just a few non-Western members of the Wedding Party:

Islam: *Hattabin* is not unlike groomsmen—male friends or family members who help the groom get ready for the wedding and support him during the ceremony.

Judaism: *Shushavim* is close family and friends who assist The Couple with wedding preparations. Though there is often no formal Wedding Party, they perform many of the same functions. Among these is holding the poles of the *huppah* (the canopy) during the ceremony.

Eastern Orthodoxy: *Koumbaros* (*koumbara*, if a female) act as the groom's Best Man. This role entails many duties and is symbolically important in the religious rite of marriage, crowning The Couple, and performing other ceremonial duties. Also assisting the Groom are the *vratimi* who act as Groomsmen and assist the *koumbaros* with his duties.

Traditional Chinese Weddings: "A Good Luck Woman"—one who has a good marriage, hale and hearty children, and living parents, will hold a red umbrella (red is the color of good luck) over the Bride's head when she leaves her home with her Groom to go to his home.

On-Line Resources

I have repeatedly stated that this book is not a wedding planner, as such.

However, knowing that you will most likely need some resources on wedding planning, I have listed a few of the better websites to help you. And for those of you who prefer wedding planning information in print form, many of these sites offer downloadable and printable checklists, as well as eBooks and paperbacks you can purchase.

Please note that these links are live in the eBook edition of this book, and while all websites listed herein are accurate at the time of publication, they may change in the future or cease to exist. I have listed these websites for informational purposes and their inclusion does not imply endorsement of the sites entire contents or of their activities.

(In alphabetical order)

www.bridalguide.com

www.brides.com

www.confetti.co.uk — United Kingdom

www.mywedding.com

www.ourwedding.com

www.theknot.com

www.weddingwindow.com

www.weddingwire.com

www.wedsite.com

About the Author

For over forty years, J. Thomas Steele has helped countless Brides, Grooms, and members of the Wedding Party write both vows and wedding speeches. His son's engagement encouraged him to "help others help themselves" by writing this book and the others in *The Wedding Series*.

Mr. Steele has an eclectic range of interests, from history and philosophy to food and children's stories, and hopes to share this enthusiasm for both learning and a good tale with his readers. He lives in South Florida and writes both fiction and non-fiction.

For more information about J. Thomas Steele, please visit his author page on Amazon's Author Central page at: amazon.com/author/jthomassteele

Like him on Facebook at:
www.facebook.com/jthomassteele.author

www.ingramcontent.com/pod-product-compliance
Lightning Source LLC
Chambersburg PA
CBHW070801240726
48654CB00007B/161